FUN AND FREEDOM

FUN AND FREEDOM
The story of an RDA group

Francesca Bullock

First published in 1995
by Starr Line

© The Horsley RDA Groups

Composed by Keele University Press,
Staffordshire, and printed by
Hartnolls, Bodmin, England

Fun and Freedom: The Story of an RDA Group

ISBN 0 95227 471 X

*All the proceeds from the sale of this book go
to the Horsley RDA Groups.*

Contents

Introduction   11

1. The Summer of '68   14
2. From Royalty to the Recession   18
3. The Driving Force   23
4. Persuasion and Progress   29
5. 'Hello Miss'   35
6. A Woman of Substance   43
7. Beech Nut and Friends   47
8. Tina's First Ride   51
9. A Helping Hand   54
10. Riding to Remission   58
11. Summer Holidays   61
12. Medical Opinion   97
13. Fund Raising   100
14. Driving for the Disabled   105
15. The 'Ben Hurs'   112
16. Donkeys and Dreams   118
17. The Real Heroes   122
18. A View From Both Sides   127
19. Special Events   132
20. Jubilee Celebrations   137
21. Progress with International Driving Trials   139
22. Driving into the Future   144
23. The Future   146

Appendix   148

Acknowledgements

This is a true story about people. Ordinary people. A story of remarkable courage, tenacity, determination and enthusiasm. It involves many emotions – hope, happiness, sadness and achievement. Confidence was everywhere, creating an electricity and excitement that would fill the air. So much success offset the inevitable failures and occasional tragedy. It is all about life and living.

Many people came regularly to help, week after week, in sunshine of course but also in snow, ice, rain or fog – whatever the weather or other problems they never let down their disabled friends.

I knew so many of these people. That is why I was so delighted when asked by the Horsley Group to put together this remarkable story of the first 25 years.

There are so many people to thank and ponies to remember, that a list of them all would be far too long. We have done our best in some of the Appendices but here I must mention three.

Stella, my late wife, who really began it all and then shepherded our groups and so many others along so unstintingly that I know it contributed to shortening her life. Yet today, up and down the country I still hear people talking about her with affection, remembering the help and advice she gave them.

Finally, John and Francesca Bullock for their additional careful research and without whose help the story would never have been written.

Ron Hancock

 BUCKINGHAM PALACE.

New ideas often look obvious once they have been introduced. Disabled people can now take part in many sports, but it was not always possible for them to do so. Riding for the disabled was a late starter and I am quite sure that there were many who said it could not be done. Then along came a group of enthusiasts at West Horsley and demonstrated how successful it could be.

When I first started carriage driving in 1972, I was aware that Riding for the Disabled Groups were being formed in various parts of the country. It seemed to me that, at least for some disabled people, driving might be even more appropriate. Once again the West Horsley Group took up the idea and proved that it could work, and now driving has been taken up by some hundred RDA Groups all over the country.

It is evident that this book has been very carefully researched and the author has brought out just how much this new activity has meant for so many disabled people. This has made the book highly interesting in its own right, but it is also a most valuable record of the beginning and development of a new idea.

Introduction

"When horse and rider each can trust the other everywhere ... For the one will do what the other demands ... and when it is done, they can live through a run that neither could face alone."

Rudyard Kipling, 'Together' (England at War)

As soon as Paul saw the pony he became animated and motivated to do something. His customary vacant stare was replaced by a spark of anticipation and once he was mounted on the pony and walking it was plain to see what riding was doing for this eight year old autistic boy who was usually so cut off from the outside world and those around him.

* * *

Riding is generally considered one of the most dangerous sports, a feeling emphasised by the fatalities which have occurred in the sport in recent years. Yet the same activity also has a tremendous therapeutic value and brings pleasure to thousands of mentally and physically handicapped people in Britain and abroad.

Mentally handicapped children and adults, to whom the outside world can be a dark tunnel, find comfort in their contact with a horse or pony which neither expects or demands anything from them. This encourages them to display the responsiveness they often find impossible to show to other people, even their closest family. The benefits are both physical and psychological. The sense of achievement felt by a disabled person while riding is often the first such feeling they have ever experienced and gives them the confidence to attempt other activities. Acquiring a skill which many able bodied people do not have also produces a feeling of pride and a desire to improve. It is an activity in which they are treated as people and not patients. They are accepted as riders and, as a result, accept the people around them, learning to communicate and express their feelings.

For many, communication can be a constant source of frustration, in possession of a bright and inquiring mind but trapped in a body they can't control and unable to speak. Riding, and the desire to control the horse, illustrates clearly how much they understand as they respond to commands from the instructors and helpers. In the same way, the lazy and unresponsive find a sense of purpose and the enjoyment of riding produces the effort which many refuse, or are unable, to apply in other areas of their lives.

From a physical aspect the warmth transmitted by a horse encourages stiff and unyielding muscles to relax; the motion of riding helps to strengthen back and neck muscles, straighten limbs and improve balance.

Those riders whose ability is limited by their physical handicap nevertheless benefit from the sheer fun of sitting on a horse and experiencing the world from a greater height. Confined to a wheelchair, riding gives them a chance to look down on other people and feel tall. The experience of riding across a field or along a track, looking over hedgerows and watching wildlife, something which most able bodied people take for granted, provides an all too brief respite from the 'prison' of wheelchair or crutches. To those who progress sufficiently to be able to ride without helpers or leaders, the sense of freedom produced by trotting, or even cantering, on a horse is priceless. It is the only freedom and independence that many of them have; riding gives them the opportunity to cover an area they couldn't possibly negotiate on their feet.

Those prevented from riding by their weight or disability can experience the same feeling of freedom by carriage driving, a sport in which they can participate from the security of their wheelchairs and in many cases develop a high degree of skill.

The value of riding to disabled people was first recognised at the turn of the century by Dame Agnes Hunt, founder of the first orthopaedic hospital at Oswestry in 1901, and by Olive Sands, who during the First World War took her horses to the Oxford hospital where men wounded in France faced rejection for further army service. During the 1950s and 60s the possibilities of riding for all types of handicaps were explored, most notably for the victims of the polio epidemic of that time.

Further inspiration and encouragement was provided by the Danish rider Liz Hartel, who won a silver medal in the dressage event at the Helsinki Olympic Games in spite of being partially paralysed in both legs and unable to walk without the aid of crutches.

In 1964 the British Horse Society's Advisory Council on Riding for the Disabled was formed, with eight groups in Britain providing riding for disabled people. Five year later the number of groups had reached 80 and the Riding for the Disabled Association had replaced the Advisory Council. In 1974 the RDA included driving for those who were unable to ride but enjoyed the contact with horses and now, nearly 20 years later, there are more than 700 groups providing riding or driving to thousands of disabled people all over Britain as well as 40 overseas.

With the help of thousands of volunteers, and under the presidency of Her Royal Highness The Princess Royal, the RDA provides a valuable extra dimension to the lives of many who would otherwise have little or no form of recreation. Most important of all, riding and driving have brought the handicapped out and removed the cotton wool with which society so often surrounds them.

The late Dame Georgina Buller, founder of the St Loyes College at Exeter and Queen Elizabeth's College at Leatherhead for the training of the disabled, spoke for handicapped people everywhere when she said: "Normality is the goal to which every disabled person, without exception, passionately aspires, and which all in their degrees can achieve if given the right opportunities and encouragement."

This book tells the story of an RDA group in Surrey which was founded in 1969 to give the handicapped the chance to take part in an activity enjoyed by so many able bodied people. Inevitably the terms 'disabled' and 'handicapped' appear frequently but these are descriptive and not intended as a means of classification. This is not a story about the disabled, it is about people.

Chapter One
The Summer of '68

As nine year old Ann-Marie Hancock watched the display by handicapped riders from the Cranleigh based group of Riding for the Disabled at the local county show, she had an idea which was to bring a new world within reach of thousands of handicapped people in Surrey. Why not use her pony Beech Nut to give a disabled child the fun and pleasure of riding? She had noticed Paul Creswell in church and felt that the eight year old autistic boy would be the ideal pupil. Her mother Stella Hancock agreed and, on a lovely September day in 1968, Paul arrived at Hillside Farm with his mother Ann, to take the first steps towards the start of the West Horsley Group of the Riding for the Disabled Association.

Ann Creswell takes up the story: "Our eldest son was highly active and could not sit at a desk, so we started to take him riding, as I felt that if he could learn to control a horse he'd have to control himself. While visiting some friends in Wales who had ponies I asked them if we could try putting Paul on a pony as well, as we had great trouble communicating with him and I had noticed that the larger the animal he came in contact with, the more relaxed he became. We never had to wonder whether he would enjoy the prospect of riding as the next day, while we were preparing to put his brother on the pony, Paul's foot appeared from the other side and so we quickly put him in the saddle.

"His enjoyment was immediately obvious but when we returned home we couldn't ask a riding school to give him lessons as very little was known at the time about autism. Even to the initiated it suggested wild, uncontrollable behaviour, and we knew from bitter experience that we had to be very careful who we chose to teach Paul. Stella Hancock's suggestion that we brought him over to Hillside to meet Beech Nut was the answer to my prayers.

"We began by walking up and down the long drive. To begin with we felt it necessary to have one person leading the pony and one either side of Paul, so Stella, Ann-Marie and I would all accompany him, which was a bit of a crowd with a small pony. Gradually we progressed to the fields and woods and I felt safe taking Paul out by myself. He didn't have any problem with sitting on a pony – he had extraordinary balance – or any worry about falling off. I was leading him through the woods one day and turned round to see Paul face down in the leaves, totally unperturbed by his tumble.

"Riding helped him to communicate and become more aware of his surroundings. He became more alert and responsive and, although at first this didn't produce any verbal response, he did respond to demands to kick his pony on, sit up, use the rein, and even undertook the various exercises with a great deal of laughter. His first words were spoken while riding. He learnt the names of the ponies – Beech Nut and Mousie – and when Dimple arrived he learnt other words as well. Dimple tended to throw his head up and down and this made Paul aware of a mouth on the other end of the reins. Quite naturally, and without being told, he 'gave and took' with his hands and could on occasions be heard to say 'steady Dimple', or 'trot on Dimple', or 'stop, you're pulling'."

Stella Hancock's zeal was not satisfied by Paul Creswell's solo rides and her suggestion to Ann Creswell that they should start a group to provide riding for other disabled children met with an equally enthusiastic response. Although without a horsey background, Ann visited one of the first established groups, at Chingford in Essex, and returned full of ideas.

In the autumn of 1969 Ron and Stella Hancock went to the National Equestrian Centre at Stoneleigh in Warwickshire to meet Caroline Haynes, the secretary of the Advisory Council on Riding for the Disabled. Armed with her advice they held a meeting at Hillside Farm on November 26th. The 51 people present included the divisional medical officer of health, the chief paediatrician from St Thomas's Hospital, founder members of the neighbouring Cranleigh group, representatives of the Red Cross, Infant Welfare health visitors, and experts from the youth service, medical and horse worlds. A committee was formed which had its first meeting two weeks later, and the West Horsley Group of the Riding for the Disabled was on its way.

The idea of using horse riding as a form of exercise and therapy for handicapped people was still relatively unexplored and the group's first problem was finding clients. One school in Guildford dismissed the idea because they said their pupils were "not in the financial range to be able to go riding". Although offered riding for their pupils free of charge the school could not be persuaded. Some parents were equally apprehensive, considering their children very fragile and horses too dangerous.

An approach to Hatchford Park, the Inner London Educational Authority's top residential school for the handicapped, at Cobham, also met with a cool response from the headmaster Mr Hughes, who mistrusted what he thought of as 'do-gooder' ladies. He didn't want the children in his care to become involved with something that he felt would soon fizzle out. The persistence of Ron and Stella Hancock and

Ann Creswell eventually won him over and he agreed to send a few pupils to begin riding. With Sue Parker as organiser and Carol Riley in charge of the helpers, a small band of volunteers was collected, together with four reliable, quiet ponies for the first session, which was held at Hillside on Tuesday May 5th 1970.

Kath Stevens was one of the first approached by Stella Hancock in her search for suitable ponies and Conker, a chestnut Welsh cross arab was duly recruited, having shown his patience and willingness to cope with Kath's children climbing all over him. As Kath recalls, that inaugural lesson established a pattern which was to grow in leaps and bounds.

"Our first meeting was fairly hectic. I rode Conker over to Hillside Farm, which is about a mile away across the Sheepleas. It took a little time to sort out children, ponies and helpers. The children were very apprehensive to begin with but as they came to know us and the ponies they settled down and looked forward to their next lesson. It was wonderful to see them progress, not only with their riding but in their personalities as well. The children who spent most of their time in a wheelchair seemed to achieve a certain independence from sitting on top of a living creature and often acquired a great sense of balance.

"When the weather was fine we used to take them for a ride into the Sheepleas and had great fun riding around the paths and woods. As most of the children came from the London area they were thrilled to be in the countryside and close to nature. They learned quite a lot about plants as well as we used to have treasure hunts collecting wild flowers and so on."

Tuesday afternoons became the regular time for the group to meet and two weeks after that first lesson Paul Creswell was joined by seven pupils from Hatchford Park. As Ann Creswell explains, the contact with others added a new dimension to Paul's riding. "In his own quiet way Paul benefited enormously from riding with disabled companions – doing things with others, observing them out of the corner of his eye – and he would often make comments on the lessons, not at the time but usually in the evening or the next day. Riding not only brought the disabled into contact with each other but also gave the parents of disabled children the chance to meet and share their problems. There was very little help available at that time for the families of handicapped children and it was very useful to talk to others in similar circumstances.

"Paul's acceptance of other children and the other instructors and helpers came as a great relief. We were outside which helped, because in a room he would probably have felt more threatened. That opened our eyes. People were prepared to make allowances and he picked up the friendly vibes and responded to them. We had found something that he accepted and where he in turn was accepted."

The early sessions at Hillside took place in a small barn, the floor of which had been levelled by a group of volunteers from the Surrey Association of Youth Clubs, led by John Collier, and Terry Thompson, a methodist clergyman who had been seconded to PHAB (Physically handicapped and able bodied). The original floor was dug up and replaced with sand and woodchips; bales formed the walls and, despite limited space, the group flourished. That winter the interior of the barn was painted white and lights were fitted which enabled the lessons to continue through the months when darkness fell early.

In May 1971 a class was started for 12 mentally handicapped adolescents from the Pond House Training Centre near Guildford, and in September of that year a Thursday morning ride began for three mentally handicapped children brought by their mothers, a number that soon doubled. Support for the West Horsley group grew in the form of volunteers, helpers and donations and when the first annual general meeting was held in November 1971 the committee was able to report on a healthy situation. A total of 247 rides had taken place, ten children had passed the RDA Test One and eight had passed Test Two; thanks to tremendous fundraising efforts the financial basis was sound and further expansion was planned.

By February 1973 it became clear that the group had outgrown Hillside Farm and needed to find suitable facilities elsewhere. The solution was provided by June and Ray Childs, who had considered starting their own RDA group but instead offered the use of their indoor school and riding school ponies at Wyvenhoe in Bookham to the West Horsley. The establishment of a permanent base for the group coincided with the inclusion of riding in the curriculum at Hatchford Park, where a rota was set up to give all the children a chance to ride. Mr Hughes' original doubts had been dispelled and he became one of the group's staunchest supporters. Hatchford Park was the school chosen by the London County Council to show leading foreign visitors the latest methods that were being used to teach the disabled. The West Horsley Group of the RDA now had an official seal of approval.

Chapter Two
From Royalty to the Recession

By 1974 the West Horsley had 56 regular riders, including one from the School for the Blind in Leatherhead, but it was not all plain sailing. Ron Hancock, who as chairman was sometimes the only man at committee meetings, wrote: "Progress is slow, patience is essential, tenacity is astonishing." The move to Wyvenhoe did, however, simplify the organisation of the rides as there were now enough suitable ponies 'on site' to cope with the number of riders and the indoor school provided more space than the barn at Hillside.

That year the Variety Club of Great Britain presented the RDA with five portable tack rooms, the first of which was received by the West Horsley and erected at Wyvenhoe. The tack room was officially opened by Princess Anne on October 23rd and provided the group with somewhere to gather on cold, wet days. This enabled stable management sessions to begin, which gave the children the chance to learn about grooming, the different parts of a saddle and bridle, types of feed and basic points of the horse. The lessons proved very popular as the children enjoyed learning more about the ponies they loved.

While riding provided an ideal form of therapy for many disabled people it proved beyond the scope of many others for whom the contact with animals nevertheless provided considerable enjoyment. In 1974 the Sandhurst RDA group had started a driving section using donkeys and a visit to the group by Stella Hancock and fellow driving enthusiasts Felicity Andrews and Sarah Garnett led to the formation in 1977 of the West Horsley driving section, which got underway on a Wednesday afternoon in May with four drivers and four ponies.

The year 1977 will be remembered for Queen Elizabeth II's Silver Jubilee, which was marked by a variety of events and celebrations around the country, including a drive organised by the British Driving Society to raise money for newly designed vehicles to be used by RDA groups. An appeal was also launched by the Prince of Wales to "encourage and enable young people to work together to help others of all ages in the community; to make available as soon as possible after the close of the appeal, grants to meet specific and needed youth projects throughout Great Britain, the Channel Islands and the Isle of Man; to support projects for the benefit of young people of all Commonwealth countries; to give much needed help to existing voluntary youth organisations who are in dire need of funds and who, due to inflation, may have had to curtail or abandon worthwhile projects."

The projects and activities to be supported by the Queen's Silver Jubilee Appeal included service to the disabled or handicapped. Projects and proposals were submitted to local district councils for consideration, among them an ambitious plan for expansion from the West Horsley Group of the RDA. One again it was Stella Hancock who took the initiative and produced the outline for the Surrey Youth Involvement Committee to consider at their meeting in December. The two phase project included the establishment of an independent ride at Wyvenhoe for some of the disabled sent by the Lockwood Centre who had progressed well enough to ride without helpers. Wyvenhoe agreed to charge them at the children's rate of £2.50 per lesson and the new advanced ride would enable the RDA to take on additional handicapped riders. The second phase involved the start of an evening session for young disabled adults who worked during the day.

The scheme met with the approval of the committee who then sent recommendations to the Lord Lieutenant's Coordinating Committee for the final decisions. Keen to set their plans in motion, the West Horsley went ahead with the launch of an advanced ride outside the auspices of the RDA for 24 of the most capable riders from Lockwood, which gave them even greater scope for improvement. It was seen as a major breakthrough and a delighted Stella Hancock reported: "This has been the most rewarding step forward for all those working in the group. Not every rider will be able to achieve these dizzy heights but we must aim to let them all enjoy their riding to the full, and this must surely be attained through achievement."

The second phase of the project, to provide riding for young handicapped people in full time employment, started on the evening of Wednesday July 12th 1978 with girls from the Grange Training Centre and Workshop for the Disabled in Little Bookham. They were later joined by residents of Dorincourt in Leatherhead who worked full time at the Queen Elizabeth's Training Centre. Helpers for the Wednesday evening sessions were provided by the Howard of Effingham Comprehensive School in Bookham and the schoolchildren happily accepted the challenge of communicating with the handicapped riders. As Stella Hancock wrote, when explaining the value of the evening ride: "Up to the age of 16 schooling and many other activities are available to occupy the daily life of the handicapped child, but after the age of 16 life can be very empty for them."

By 1979, with the addition of a self-financing ride for pupils from the Park School in Woking, the group was operating on Tuesday,

Wednesday, Thursday and Friday and the rising costs had led to the introduction of a fee of 50 pence per pupil per session. It proved to be an exciting year with four riders asked to parade at the Pony Club's Golden Jubilee, eight children invited by the Variety Club to attend a lunch at the Savoy in London held in association with Radio One, and success for the group's entry in the ridden fancy dress class at the Royal Windsor Horse Show.

Ten years after the inaugural ride the West Horsley had grown from four riders to 140, with an additional eight drivers. Riding or driving were provided on all five weekdays during the school term and the popularity of riding among the handicapped had resulted in a substantial increase in membership. After careful consideration it was decided to divide the group into four autonomous units, each with their own organisers and secretarys, to spread the load of administration. The four groups were each represented on the central committee which controlled the finances and provided a sounding board for the individual group organisers. The Tuesday rides from Hatchford Park and Pond Meadow consequently became the West Horsley 'A' Group; West Horsley 'B' took charge of the Wednesday evening rides from Dorincourt and the Grange; Wednesday, Thursday and Friday morning sessions for Lockwood, Park School and private individuals came under the auspices of West Horsley 'C', and the driving section – West Horsley 'D' – met on Monday mornings.

Due to Ray Stovold, the Master of the Chiddingfold Farmers Hunt, a welcome boost to group finances was received from the Chiddingfold Farmers Hunt Kennel Fund, whose donation of £4,000 was put into a Trust Fund, the income from which was used for the benefit of all four groups. The beginning of the eighties proved to be memorable for the West Horsley in more ways than one. On September 3rd 1980 it was finally confirmed that the group had been awarded a Queen's Silver Jubilee Certificate, which was presented on Monday December 15th 1980 at County Hall in Kingston-on-Thames by Lord Hamilton of Dalzell. The award was received on behalf of the group by Beverley Mitchell, the young instructor at Wyvenhoe who had been involved with teaching the Lockwood advanced ride. She was accompanied to County Hall by two of the handicapped riders – Shelley Harper from Dorincourt and Debra Rickman from the Grange – and group organiser Jan Richards. The appeal had raised more than £100,000 in Surrey alone, while the nationwide figure reached £16 million. The same year the group launched a newsletter called 'The Hoofpick'. Stella Hancock, together with disabled driver Neill Portsmouth and the group's pony Prince also appeared on Blue Peter promoting driving for the disabled.

The following year provided another milestone for the West Horsley with the first residential summer camp run by Yvonne Fisk for children from the Park School. Sadly, however, the group also lost one of its greatest supporters when Mr Hughes retired from his post of headmaster at Hatchford Park. Three years later the school's new headmaster made the decision to remove riding from the curriculum which was a bitter disappointment to the group and the pupils.

In 1983 the driving group took charge of its own financial affairs. With more of her time devoted to driving activities Stella Hancock, together with her husband Ron, retired from the main committee in 1984 and the following year became chairman of the national RDA Driving Committee. The West Horsley driving group took on new drivers in the form of rehabilitation patients from RAF Chessington and performed a musical drive at the National RDA Conference as well as representing the association in the Lord Mayor's Show. Under Stella Hancock's guidance the West Horsley driving section became one of the leading lights of the driving for the disabled movement. They provided a musical demonstration at the World Carriage Driving Championships in 1986, joining with drivers from eight other RDA groups, and finally achieved independent status the following year by breaking away from the three riding groups.

Without Stella Hancock's inspiration the riding side of the West Horsley floundered for a while and her death in 1988 while on holiday in Australia left a noticeable void in the driving and RDA worlds. As a tribute to her the driving group was renamed the Stella Hancock Driving Group, which is still providing hours of enjoyment for disabled drivers and is a legacy of the work undertaken by Stella Hancock during the last ten years of her life.

Two years later the West Horsley lost another of its original committee with the death of Baron Holroyd, who had served as treasurer since the group's inception in 1969 and whose expert advice over more than 20 years had ensured its financial soundness. The introduction of a new chairman, Major John Vandeleur-Boorer, in 1990 brought further changes. In order to broaden the group's local appeal and maximise its fundraising potential the West Horsley 'A', 'B', and 'C' groups were united under the banner of the Horsley Group, which now operates under three organisers for the Tuesday, Wednesday and Thursday rides. The retirement from the committee of Sybil Atherton in 1991, followed a year later by Helen Turk and Prue Goodchild, severed the final ties with the past but the group's future is still in the hands of a band of hard working and dedicated volunteers. The effects of the recession have, like everywhere else, not gone unnoticed and the riding group relies heavily on the facilities at Wyvenhoe for its survival. Wyvenhoe has adopted the DIY livery scheme which has become the financial lifeline for so many riding schools, but this has reduced the number of school horses available.

The RDA has become entrenched in rules and regulations which, while undoubtedly introduced with the best intentions, have ruled out many of the original instructors who, although lacking official qualifications, showed the willingness and determination to support the movement and gave their time for nothing. With the emphasis now on qualified instruction, which inevitably means that the instructors have to be paid, perhaps some of the fun which was so much a part of the early days of the RDA has been lost. Nevertheless, the spirit which enabled the West Horsley to start and survive for the past 25 years is still in evidence and giving the handicapped the chance to experience that special bond between man and horse which every horseman and horsewoman values so highly.

Chapter Three
The Driving Force

Princess Alice, Countess of Athlone, would undoubtedly have been very proud of Stella Florence Hancock. While visiting St Margaret's School in Bushey, Hertfordshire where the then 16 year old Stella Mathias was a pupil, the Princess told the girls to "hold on to the great Christian principles, think courageously for yourselves and not say what everyone else is saying". They were words that Stella Hancock followed throughout her life, a life in which she achieved so much through her energy and determination.

Born on September 1st 1931, the eldest of Howard and Marie Mathias's two daughters, she spent her childhood in Richmond, Surrey, where the family remained throughout the Second World War. Her father was a draper who owned a large department store and warehouse in Putney which received a direct hit during the Blitz, but it was during the war that Stella had her first taste of driving when she persuaded John Hedges, the coachman for the family business, to let her accompany him on some of his journeys around the city, occasionally taking the reins herself.

In 1948 her father's contribution to the war effort was rewarded with a CBE and Stella accompanied her parents to Buckingham Palace for the investiture. In her journal she recalled: 'Daddy was read out as Mr Arthur Mathias. Most odd!' A note on the same page reads: 'Remember! All the bravery awards came last, and what jolly fine types won them – soldiers, miners etc.' Her admiration for courage was already evident. Young Stella was also perceptive. Following the Bicentenary Thanksgiving Service at St Paul's Cathedral in 1949 she wrote: 'The Archbishop might as well have stood up and said *We want some cash*, which he said in so many more words.'

When the family moved to Plymouth Stella began a love affair with the sea and her keen interest in sailing led to a meeting with her future husband on a cold September day in 1957. Ron Hancock had served on destroyers in the Royal Navy during the war but had then resumed a successful career as an insurance broker. His talent and hard work had brought financial rewards, including an eight ton, sea going sailing cruiser which he shared with a friend and kept at Burnham-on-Crouch.

Stella was now working in London as secretary to the legal manager of the Daily Express but spent many weekends at Burnham with her sailing friends. On this particular weekend Ron was arranging for his boat to be layed up for the winter, when Stella walked into the bar and he recognised her as the same vivacious young girl that he had noticed on an earlier visit. A word with the barman enabled Ron to arrange a meeting with her that evening and three months later they announced their engagement.

Ron and Stella were married on January 18th 1958 at the Holy Trinity Church in London. Before her marriage Stella claimed to have three ambitions – to pass her driving test, to own a really fine boat and to live on a farm. The first was accomplished without any difficulty and Ron provided the second. Within a year of their marriage the third was realised when they bought Hillside Farm in West Horsley, which was to be their home for all but the last few months of their life together.

Sailing remained Ron and Stella's great hobby until soon after the birth of their first child, Ann-Marie, in 1960. A small child didn't prove to be the ideal passenger and following the birth of William in 1962 the yacht was sold. The gift of a pony and a basket saddle from a local family who were moving to Scotland launched Ann-Marie's riding career and the acquisition of a small cart rekindled Stella's love of driving. Ann-Marie's enthusiasm for riding increased as she grew older and both William and Richard , who was born in 1966, shared in the fun that the ponies provided.

Mousie, the gift pony, was followed by Twanger, Beech Nut, Dimple and Zephair. The purchase of Golden Oriel from the Welsh cob enthusiast Ursula Lees was the start of Stella's appreciation of the Welsh breed. In 1975 she joined the Welsh Pony and Cob Society and established her own breeding line with the prefix of Brynside, which is Welsh for Hillside. The youngstock were generally sold as foals although the first produce of her mare Caron Mali, named Dewi, was driven by Stella with great success in driving trials in Britain and abroad.

Both she and Ron were very proud of Ann-Marie's riding ability. With her much loved Maple Galacier she progressed through the dressage ranks and spent two years with the top German trainer Georg Theodorescu at his Warendorf establishment. The results she and 'Gally' achieved during their stay in Germany put them among the top 15 combinations in Europe and after returning to England they were strongly tipped to win the 1988 National Championships. Sadly, Gally inexplicably ground to a halt in the middle of their test and was discovered the next day to have broken a pastern, which was inoperable.

Stella's own riding exploits had ended literally with a thud. While out hunting her horse shied at a rabbit, unseating Stella who fell on top of the startled animal. The unfortunate rabbit did not recover and, although happily unhurt, Stella never rode again.

The launch of the West Horsley Riding for the Disabled group provided an outlet for Stella's considerable energy and enthusiasm. Always looking for new challenges, the initial objections to the idea voiced by schools, parents and doctors were simply fuel to her determination to make the venture a success. "Stella was marvellous," recalls Sue Parker. "When we were trying to find clients she liaised with everyone and persuaded the Surrey County Council to support us. She was an inspiration."

Stella's great gift was her ability to see the positive side rather than the problems. She concentrated on the abilities of the handicapped rather than their disabilities and was always looking for things they could do rather than those they couldn't. The RDA tests were, she felt, of great importance and she always organised ceremonies for the handing out of certificates and badges to emphasise the sense of achievement felt by the disabled riders.

With the acceptance of riding as an activity for the disabled, she was given a fresh challenge in 1974 when Princess Anne arrived to open the tack room donated by the Variety Club. During the short car journey from the Royal helicopter to Wyvenhoe, the Princess mentioned to Ron and Stella that her father Prince Philip was keen that the handicapped should be given an opportunity to drive as well as ride.

Stella didn't need any further encouragement. Driving had been added to the RDA's constitution and the disabled were already driving donkeys at Sandhurst with Nancy Pethick but Stella wanted her disabled to use ponies to experience fully the fun and excitement of driving. Ignoring the objections of some senior members of the British Driving Society who felt that it was far too dangerous for the disabled, she established a driving section using quiet, reliable ponies. Her attitude was never irresponsible, however, and safety together with enjoyment was always her top priority. "We cannot make it 100% safe," she said, "but 90% is acceptable. That 10% is, I dare say, where the 'fun aspect' for some handicapped drivers comes in."

After the launch of the driving section of the West Horsley RDA group in 1977 Stella began to work untiringly on a national basis, gathering support and helping to organise demonstrations and events. Driving in West Horsley continued to flourish and Hillside Farm was always a hive of activity during one of her disabled driving rallies. With the fields crowded with driving vehicles and the drivers either under instruction or enjoying a drive around the farm and surrounding woods, Stella would be in her element organising food for everyone or dashing outside to take on of the lessons.

The happy atmosphere at Hillside contributed to the success of all Stella's ventures. The large, friendly kitchen was often full of people, either helpers or disabled people sitting in the warmth while waiting for their turn to ride or drive. Everyone always seemed to be enjoying themselves and it was Stella's gift for making life seem fun which made her such a popular figure.

"Stella was an amazing person," recalls fellow driver Sarah Garnett. "Not only could she drag you into doing anything but she also ensured that you ended up enjoying yourself as well. I used to find myself rushing around like mad, getting utterly exhausted, while Stella drove around in her car organising everything. But she had a marvellous way of dealing with people and so I never minded.

"I judged a disabled driving class for her one day and when I pointed out afterwards that some of the ponies were not really obedient enough for driving, she said, 'Right. I'm going to organise a driving for the disabled conference and you can explain how to school a pony properly for driving.' That was typical of Stella."

"If she asked you to do things, you did them," agrees Felicity Andrews, with whom Stella founded the driving section. "She was the world's A1 delegator and so clever because she knew the right people to ask for help. Her great forte was getting things up and running."

Stella's 'Ben Hurs', as she called her disabled drivers, became a major part of her life. They didn't want pity and she understood that. What they wanted was help and encouragement and this is just what Stella gave them. Neil Portsmouth, one of the first handicapped drivers in Britain, acknowledges the debt that he and many other disabled people owe her. "Stella, probably more than anyone, changed the direction of my life. She was a great one for asking people what they would like to achieve and then doing her best to make it happen. I did things I never thought were possible, thanks to Stella. She was a great catalyst; wherever Stella was things happened around her – she made them happen. She knew the right people to approach and wasn't afraid to fight on our behalf, even if it upset some people. Because she believed in you, she would make other people give you a chance. She opened the doors for us to go in and prove what we could do."

The willingness to fight on behalf of her disabled friends occasionally led to friction between Stella and other sections of the horse world but she was never afraid to ruffle a few feathers in the course of helping others. She was always anxious that, despite their handicaps, all her 'Ben Hurs' should have the opportunity to compete as far as possible on level terms with able bodied drivers. One of the main problems was the vehicles. The Jubilee cart which had been designed to take a wheelchair and an able bodied passenger sitting alongside, lacked style and was often referred to affectionately as a 'tea chest on wheels'. In 1984 Stella persuaded the Worshipful Company of Coachmakers and Coach Harnessmakers to sponsor a competition to find a new design, and the winning Jackson Darent revolutionised driving for disabled people all over the world. Even The Princess Royal succumbed happily to Stella's unique brand of charm and persuasion by taking one of the new vehicles with her in the baggage compartment of the aircraft flying her to the Far East, dropping it off at Singapore for the newly formed driving for the disabled group on the island.

It was typical of Ron and Stella that, during the trip to Singapore, Australia, America and Canada that they planned together in 1988, time should be set aside to visit as many disabled driving groups as possible in order to give them help and advice. In Singapore, Stella spent the day giving driving lessons and instruction to helpers who were new to the task and valued her wealth of experience. Despite getting drenched during a series of heavy storms followed by spells of very hot sun making everything steam, she insisted on continuing until the end of the afternoon, returning to the hotel completely exhausted. Her tragic and untimely death in Australia a few days later shocked her family and friends and left a void in many lives. The change of name to the Stella Hancock Driving Group will ensure that her memory lives. A memorial service at the Holy Trinity Church in Brompton Road was attended by more than 650 friends and leading members of the horse world including Sir Brian McGrath, representing Prince Philip.

Millie Millington, a member of the West Horsley Driving Group since 1983, later summed up the feelings of many when she said: "Dear Stella was our dynamic driving force and our greatest loss. The greatest tribute we can give her is to ensure that the group goes from strength to strength."

When asked why she spent so much time working on behalf of the disabled, Stella's reply was always: "I wish I could do more. We should all try and help those less fortunate than ourselves and I have been so fortunate in my life and have so much to be thankful for. Those Ben Hurs mean a great deal to me."

There is no doubt that she also meant a great deal to a great many people and to all her 'Ben Hurs' Stella Hancock WAS disabled driving. The following letter which appeared in the RDA News shortly after her death illustrates the affection which she inspired in those she helped and the legacy she left behind.

'It was with great sadness and shock that I heard of the sudden death of Stella Hancock in Australia in February. As one of her 'Ben Hurs' I shall always remember the kindness, encouragement and support that she gave to us all. She always managed to get you to do that little bit more than you thought you could, not because you had to, but because in that special way that Stella had, she made you want to try harder. She always made us feel proud of what we were doing.

'Those of us that were lucky enough to be asked to take part in the musical drive at the World Championships at Ascot will remember the bumpy rehearsals in the car park opposite the racecourse – performing it over and over again until we got it right "for Stella". One of the many things that Stella gave to Driving for the Disabled was the feeling that if we were going to do something then we should do it well and do it right. What we mustn't do now that Stella is no longer with us is to let our standards slip. Stella can never be replaced, but her 'Ben Hurs' can carry on with the high standards that she set. So perhaps the next time we go into the dressage arena or drive around the cones, let's think "for Stella". Or maybe even just at our group meetings, try to hold the reins that bit better, or just make more effort to sit up that little bit straighter. Let's think to ourselves, this is "for Stella". That way Driving for the Disabled will continue to improve, which is what she would have wanted more than anything. I will say this quite simply: "For Stella, with love, Ben Hur".'

Chapter Four
Persuasion and Progress

In the early days of the West Horsley RDA group, riding with disabled people was still a relatively new venture and the disabled themselves suffered from segregation. As Paula Stebbings, who became chief instructor in 1973, recalls, she and her colleagues had no previous experience to fall back on. "We hadn't come across disabled people before and we just treated them as normal beginners. It gave the parents great pleasure to see perfectly ordinary people who were used to horses and ponies, accept their handicapped children and not treat them any differently because of their disability."

Prue Goodchild, one of the group's first instructors, also stresses that from the very beginning the disabled pupils were not looked upon any differently to other aspiring riders. "We treated them just like normal children and taught them how to sit properly on a pony and so on. As long as the doctor said it was alright for them to ride, the less we know what they could and couldn't do, the better. All our riders had to have permission from their doctor to ride and we were told if there was something that they shouldn't do."

The physically handicapped sometimes ride on a large sheepskin to prevent chafing, or use a Western saddle which provides greater comfort than an ordinary saddle. Ted Leahy, a former chairman of the West Horsley and owner of Bridleways saddlery in Guildford, devised a webbing belt to be worn around the rider's waist with a handle on each side for the helpers to hold on to. This not only gives the rider confidence but also prevents them being pulled off balance by the helpers grabbing their clothing. Foot reins, enabling the pony to be steered by the rider's feet, and handles on the pommel of the saddle are also used in some cases but the majority of riders prefer to ride as normally as possible.

Learning to ride involves a certain degree of risk for anyone and although everything is done to minimise the likelihood of accidents, the value of riding to most disabled people is the challenge and fun it provides. While care must obviously be taken over those with brittle bones, it is often merely a lack of coordination and balance which makes them more vulnerable than the able bodied.

June Childs, who gave the West Horsley a lifeline 20 years ago with the facilities of Wyvenhoe riding school and still teaches the disabled on an individual basis, believes that instructing the disabled is really a matter of common sense. "You must be aware of their problems and you've got to know what they are capable of doing. But it you teach anyone to ride you know what they can do and if they're likely to be able to do more in six months time. You are always trying to achieve a fraction more but if you overstep the mark then you backtrack immediately to rebuild confidence."

One well used axiom in riding is the importance of getting back in the saddle as soon as possible after a fall and June recalls one young Downs Syndrome girl who, after taking two lessons to be persuaded to get on the pony, progressed well enough to take part in dressage competitions. A fall at one show left her with a broken arm and her mother brought her to Wyvenhoe with her arm still in plaster so that she could begin to rebuild her confidence immediately by walking on a quiet pony. When the plaster was removed she was raring to go again, whereas a long break without riding might have resulted in a return of her first lesson nerves.

June Childs' daughter, now Leslie Campbell, also teaches the disabled at Wyvenhoe and tries to follow as normal a teaching routine as possible. "You can't demand too much but it is important to keep repeating instructions when teaching the mentally handicapped and vary the lesson as much as possible. Some handicapped riders have surprised me with their progress. When they arrive they can't even walk to the school, but then you see them riding and realise that their bodies are working – it's amazing."

Progress can be difficult to measure and if some disabled people never become proficient in the saddle, the same is true of many able bodied adults, as Leslie points out. "You can take an older, able bodied person and teach them to sit on a quiet horse and enjoy a gentle hack, but you'll never make a rider out of them. The same is true of many disabled people."

Successful teaching in any sphere requires a rapport between student and teacher. Communication is vital and it is this factor which at times makes instructing the mentally handicapped difficult. Riding has shown, however, that it is not an insurmountable problem, as June Childs explains. "The mentally handicapped are very childlike and you have to talk to them on their own level. At Wyvenhoe we teach a lot of children and teach them in a different way to adults. It can take several weeks to get the trust of a mentally handicapped pupil but they are very loving and, once you have their confidence, very loyal. As they get more used to you, you can change the terms that you use when teaching them and it is very rewarding when they learn a new movement because they are so thrilled.

"Sometimes they seem totally oblivious to what you are saying and then you have to be quite firm. If you get frustrated or lose your temper then you might as well give up, but that applies to teaching anyone. It is very good for the mentally handicapped to use their brains and they can easily become institutionalised. One boy came here with a disabled group but also rode individually with an able bodied class. He appeared quite handicapped when with the disabled group but talked non-stop when with his able bodied friends and was really quite an intelligent lad. Riding does help the children to develop their personalities. They'll come into the school and tell me what they've been doing and what they're going to do. I can't always understand them but the great thing is they try."

The limited retentive ability of the mentally handicapped is sometimes a barrier to improvement, particularly as riders with the group only ride for half an hour, once a week. Those who have received individual tuition on a more regular basis have shown greater progress but practice is the key to success in any sport. Many people are tempted to help the disabled too much, something which Sarah Garnett, another of the West Horsley's earliest instructors, always tried to discourage. "Some disabled are quite crafty and soon learn that if they do something wrong or seem not to understand, then it will be done for them. A simple command to shorten their reins might be difficult for some but I don't mind if they only shorten one rein or shorten them two inches instead of six, as long as they do it themselves."

Sarah's initial experience with teaching the disabled was with the mentally handicapped from the Lockwood Centre and she soon decided that actions spoke louder than words. "Standing in the middle of the school and giving instructions was no use," she explains. "The only way I could get the riders' attention was by individual contact with each person. This involved a lot of running as I had to physically show them how to rise to the trot by pushing them up and down in the saddle as the pony trotted round."

The secret of teaching lies in encouraging the pupil's desire to learn. The strength of riding is the contact with an animal, to which children in particular respond. A number of children who have been previously withdrawn and incommunicative have, like Paul Creswell, begun to talk as a result of their rapport with a horse or pony and their willingness to learn stems from a wish to control the animal.

Producing speech from a normally silent child is seen as a major breakthrough and the therapeutic effect of riding far outweighs the importance of the level of riding achieved. Helen Turk, who spent nearly 20 years as a group organiser and instructor with the West Horsley, derived tremendous satisfaction from her pupils' reaction to riding. "Obviously it's nice to teach people to improve," she says, "but you start to feel pleased with small things. Although their riding doesn't necessarily progress, they often improve in other ways, particularly communication. One can get awfully depressed if you feel that they haven't enjoyed it and really pleased if they have. It is difficult sometimes when you think that you have gone as far as you can with a rider and you wonder whether it might be better to stop and give their place to someone who's never had the chance to ride. But is it more important to spend time with someone who could perhaps learn to ride quite well, than help someone who won't make any more progress but really enjoys riding and receives tremendous therapeutic value from it?"

Helen's wide experience with the disabled has shown her the importance of balancing an awareness of a rider's handicap with a need to encourage progress. "I went on an RDA course for instructors and as part of our training we had to ride a horse while blindfolded to understand the sensations that blind people experience. It affects your balance and that knowledge helped me when I was teaching a blind person who had once had sight. Sometimes, however, it can be better not to know if a rider has a certain handicap. If, for example, they have something wrong with their left hand it is often better for them to try and use it, but if you are aware of it you will probably tell them to use their right hand instead."

While the majority of disabled riders progress to trotting, relatively few have the necessary balance to cope with cantering. "It is such a big movement and they find it very unseating," explains Helen. "Not many of the riding school horses can canter slowly and if they are stiff it can be very uncomfortable. The riders all tend to want to gallop and jump, but if the horse does break into a canter they are usually terrified. However, if you say 'well done, you've cantered' they are so pleased that they forget to be frightened."

Surprisingly perhaps, most handicapped riders adapt to jumping more easily than cantering. The fences may be only small but the sense of achievement is considerable. "If you are clever," says Paula Stebbings, "you can build a fence of crossed poles which looks quite big but is in fact small in the middle of the fence where the pony jumps."

To vary the lessons, games and races are included, many of which are educational, such as the posting game which helps to teach the children to read. Different shapes and pictures are used for those unable to read and this adds a new dimension to an instructor's role. Paula Stebbings was once asked by an interested spectator if she was a kindergarten teacher.

In the early days the West Horsley was advised not to mix the mentally and physically handicapped riders, but as very few of their pupils have been purely physically handicapped this has never been a problem. Many of the rides vary considerably in terms of handicaps and ability which, although difficult in some ways, provides inspiration for the riders and at times help for the instructor. A group of blind riders could, for instance, be a problem but one or two blind riders fit easily into a mixed group as there is always someone to give them a lead. Half an hour can sometimes be a long time when instructing people who are limited in what they can do, but everyone can learn from others. It is always beneficial to realise that others have problems as well and disabled people find it equally inspiring to see fellow riders with different disabilities to their own. It produces a spirit of camaraderie which is heartwarming to see as they encourage each other to greater effort.

Lack of confidence affects many disabled people and can be overcome by achievement. The RDA has developed a system of tests which the riders can take as they progress, starting with stage one and culminating in the coveted gold award. These also receive full recognition by the schools and the badges and certificates awarded by the RDA groups are presented at their own end of term prizegiving, offering a 'low achiever' the chance to succeed in something that is recognised by everyone. Tears of happiness have been shed by the handicapped when they receive a certificate which is often the first thing they have ever won. The helpers are often overcome by emotion as well.

The tests include stable management questions which can provide a problem. Notes drawn up by RDA to help in the instruction of stable management dealt with different handicaps, from the physically handicapped who might find difficulty in taking bridles apart and putting them back together, to the very mentally handicapped and those unable to speak. With the physically handicapped, instructors are encouraged to allow the students to do as much as they possibly can, even if it takes a long time. It is better to offer the students the chance to attempt the exercise rather than assume that they are not going to be able to manage.

The mentally handicapped range from the educationally sub-normal (ESN) who have learning difficulties and little retentive ability, to those with whom communication is severely limited. It is important to set different goals for each student according to ability, to keep lessons short and introduce only a small amount of new material in each one. Different methods of teaching the same facts often help to reinforce the lesson, with the golden rule being 'a little at a time'. The use of visual aids, together with eliminating all unnecessary speech, can help communication with those unable to speak, who can often show their understanding by pointing or reacting to a request.

Patience and persistence are required by instructors, and June Childs recalls how she used to send the children away with parcels of feed samples and labelled pieces of grooming kit to enable their parents to test them at home. Patience is also required by the examiners, who are encouraged to look for what the children know rather than what they don't. With the mentally handicapped this often involves rephrasing questions in order to help them understand. The pupils themselves benefit tremendously from using their brains to learn more about something they find fun and interesting.

Although in recent years more emphasis has been placed on the quality of instruction, the requisites for teaching the handicapped are the same as they were 25 years ago – tolerance, patience, communication and commitment.

Keuke Kilmurry has been instructing riders from the West Horsley for 18 years. "I still get as much satisfaction and pleasure each week as I did in the early days," she says. "As an instructor of both able bodied and disabled pupils I feel that I have also benefited greatly from the experience.

"Many roads lead to Rome, as the proverb says, and I have been down a few over the years. I have had to approach any number of problems in any number of different ways, but always with the same goal in mind. If I make sure that everyone enjoys themselves, has fun and makes a little progress – however small and however long it takes – then I am happy and hopefully so are my pupils."

Chapter Five
'Hello Miss'

Whatever the physical benefits of riding to the disabled the most important aspect is the enjoyment that is provides. As Ron Hancock explains: "My recollection of visits to watch the riders was the fun. There was an extraordinary balance between the illness and disease and this tremendous amount of fun. The greatest benefit of being on horseback is to morale and there is a real need to cheer the spirits of disabled people."

It is this element of fun which encourages communication as the withdrawn respond to the contact with an undemanding animal and with the people who are helping to provide something that they enjoy. Riding is something the disabled can do that many of their able bodied friends can't. For many of the adults in particular it is their first step into a new world which helps them to go on and try other activities. Riding helps them to blossom and gives those brought up in towns and cities the chance to see the countryside, broadening the spectrum of their often restricted lives.

In the early days of the group attracting pupils was one of the biggest problems, along with continuity as the children sent by Hatchford Park were often absent due to medical examinations or operations. The reaction of parents to their children's disabilities varied considerably between those who accepted what fate had dealt them, those who tried to ignore it and those who were very defensive. Riding was looked upon by many as far too dangerous, but once they realised that the instructors and helpers were all confident and capable and saw the smiles on the children's faces when riding, they soon became keen and supportive.

In the 25 years since Paul Creswell's first ride on Beech Nut thousands of riders have passed through the West Horsley group, many leaving an indelible impression with their courage and personality. Sybil Atherton, one of the original helpers and a group organiser for nearly 20 years, recalls the warmth and affection shown by many of the children. "They would arrive in their bus, waving, and if they saw a face they recognised, they would be so pleased to see you. They would hold your hand and say 'Hello Miss'. We were always 'Miss'." Sadly many of the children came from London and the group lost contact with them once they left school and returned home.

One of the children who took part in the first official lesson, on May 5th 1970, was a tall coloured boy called Linford, who had been brought to England by his parents from their home in Nigeria and then abandoned. Despite his misfortunes he was a delightful boy, always smiling, and learnt to ride very well. Another of the group's early pupils also had an unhappy family background. Eugenia was of Persian descent and paralysed from the waist down. Her parents considered it a disgrace to have a handicapped child and kept her shut away during the holidays. Unable to use her legs, Eugenia relied on her balance to stay in the saddle but still made tremendous progress and performed a dressage display in front of Princess Anne when she came to open the tack room at Wyvenhoe in 1974.

While some of the children, particularly the smaller ones, refused to ride the majority looked forward to their weekly lessons and it soon became obvious that riding had a beneficial effect on a variety of problems. One small boy called Mark came with his mother and never spoke until one day she arrived at the stables in a state of great excitement because Mark had begun to talk about the ponies.

The enjoyment of riding provided the key. Helen suffered a heart attack as a small girl which left her paralysed down her right side. Her refusal to cooperate with the physiotherapists led them to suggest riding and although at first she would do no more than sit on the pony, she soon responded to demands to pick up her reins and use her legs. Riding became something she wanted to do and as a result she worked hard and improved considerably. When she wanted to stroke the pony she found that her floppy hand felt nice when placed on the warmth of the pony's neck and this encouraged her to use it.

The group also achieved considerable success with their riders in competitions. Tim, who suffered from cystic fibrosis, rode particularly well and in 1975 became the first West Horsley member to pass the RDA bronze award. In 1978 the south east region of the RDA held a special dressage competition at Hever Castle in Kent. International three day event rider Tessa Martin-Bird devised a dressage test for the occasion and a bronze challenge trophy was presented to the winner by Lady Astor. Tim represented the West Horsley, finishing a very honourable third, and the competition became an annual event, providing a rare chance for the disabled to compete.

Two years later another West Horsley pupil, Michael, won the Hever Castle competition and received his prize from Princess Anne. Hugh, a victim of cerebral palsy, overcame the lack of control over his arms by using foot reins, steering the pony with his feet. His skill was rewarded with a number of dressage successes and he gained great confidence from the competitions.

June Childs now teaches some individuals who have shown particular promise with the group and has achieved remarkable results with her pupils, notably Richard, who finished third in the 1992 National RDA Dressage Championships. Although mentally handicapped he learnt the test by heart – a considerable achievement that anyone who has ever lost their way in a dressage test will appreciate. "Richard's a lovely boy," says June, "and will try and charm me so that he can take things easy. He will push me as far as he dares but then he'll realise that he has overstepped the mark and so he sits up and starts to ride properly."

The popularity of riding within the schools associated with the West Horsley means that it is usually confined to one year, in order to give every pupil the chance to ride. This inevitably leads to sadness when riding is no longer part of their timetable and there was bitter disappointment in 1984 when riding was removed from the curriculum at Hatchford Park. Ann Creswell maintains that the feeling is one of anger rather than loss. "It is difficult to tell whether the times that Paul couldn't ride affected him," she says, "although he was always overjoyed to get back on a horse. Some get very angry when they have to stop riding, because something that is readily available to the able bodied is not to them. It's not really that they suffer from withdrawal symptoms, more an anger that they are being victimised."

When riding is restricted for those sent by their schools, a number of pupils are brought by their parents and continue to ride with the group. Samantha (Sam) started with the West Horsley 18 years ago at the age of seven. A slow learner and epileptic, she was brought to the lessons by her mother Janet, who felt that it was something her animal loving daughter would enjoy. Although Sam's school allowed her to take the time off every Thursday afternoon, the headmaster did not totally approve. "The school's philosophy was that their children had moderate learning difficulties rather than stressing any mental or physical disability, and they encouraged all the children to reach their potential," explains Janet. "They were concerned that the RDA categorised children as 'disabled'."

After 18 months with the RDA Stella Hancock and June Childs felt that Sam had progressed enough to ride with an able bodied class and she has never looked back. Weekly lessons at Wyvenhoe with June Childs are still a feature of her busy life and she continues to progress, having represented her area three times in the Special Olympics. The fragility with which the disabled are so often regarded was illustrated during her second Olympic appearance when her training centre, having little experience of horses, decided that cantering was too risky and insisted that she take part in the dressage competition confined to walking and trotting – a decision that made Sam "very cross".

Fortunately on the following occasion the training centre relented and Sam was able to show off all her riding ability, finished just out of the medals in fifth place. Her finest hour, however, was in 1976 when she won a sponsored showjumping event at Goodwood in aid of the RDA. The watch that was presented to her by Lord March is still one of her most treasured possessions.

Brought up in a loving environment Sam has always been encouraged to develop new skills and as Janet explains, riding was one activity in which she could excel. "Sam enjoys life and riding was another dimension where she could achieve something, whereas academically she couldn't. She has always been confident – perhaps overconfident – and riding helped her to assess situations." Although she still clearly enjoys her riding Sam never asks to ride more often, probably because she enjoys a variety of other activities. "I like to go out hacking best," she says, "and I also enjoy cantering. Sometimes I have lessons in the school and jump over trotting poles and little jumps – but I don't like big heights."

Sam is one of the lucky ones. Her parents have given her all the love and encouragement any child could want and the result is a fun loving daughter of whom any parent could be proud. It is this individual attention that is inevitably so lacking in residential schools and centres and which leads to many disabled people becoming 'institutionalised' and unwilling to exert themselves. The instruction given to each pupil when riding promotes a feeling of importance as the rider responds to the interest and attention of instructor and helpers. This can, however, occasionally backfire. Sarah Garnett recalls one boy who fell off during a lesson and was immediately surrounded by people, full of concern in case he was injured. Once back on the pony, unhurt and having clearly enjoyed all the attention, he then threw himself off a few minutes later hoping to create a similar scene.

Riding has proved to be of particular benefit to those with spina bifida and cerebral palsy and doctors have stated that the physical movement of the spine caused by sitting on a moving animal is very good for Downs Syndrome patients.

Over the years there have of course been failures. Many able bodied people give up riding after a few attempts, deciding it is not for them, and it would be unrealistic to expect a 100% success rate with the disabled. Some give up voluntarily; in other cases the handicap proves unsuited to riding or contact with an animal. One very pretty young girl was simply uncontrollable and could not be persuaded to wear a hat. Epileptics were at first treated with caution but the condition is now more controllable and riding is not considered harmful.

The first adult pupil taken on by the West Horsley did not prove to be a success either. A former patient at Stoke Mandeville, she had broken her back and was determined to ride again. Her determination, however, was equalled by her fear and, paralysed from the neck down, she was very difficult to keep upright in the saddle. Sadly the group had to accept defeat.

More recently, the Wednesday evening ride was sent a young man by the Blind Centre in Leatherhead who had been blinded as a result of a motorbike accident and also suffered brain damage. Riding was suggested in the hope that it would improve his balance and help him to walk again, and for a year he progressed well despite a tendency to lean sideways while negotiating corners. He then became impatient and frustrated at not being able to go faster and as his physical strength proved a danger to the helpers the group could no longer cope with him.

Those people disabled as a result of an accident are often more 'bolshie' than those handicapped from birth, but very often this is channelled into a fierce determination. One ex-Household Cavalry trooper had been badly injured in an accident but was determined to ride again. His resolve enabled him to do so and he went on to represent the West Horsley in the sponsored showjumping event at Goodwood.

Today the determination to overcome handicaps is as much in evidence as ever. The group encompasses a tremendous range of disabilities in children and adults. Some, like Marianne, have no obvious handicap. A car accident left her with slight brain damage and although she cannot remember riding as a child she shows natural ability. Very chatty, she always gives credit to the horse and refuses to accept any praise for her own skill.

Sharon is at the other end of the scale. Severely spastic and confined to a wheelchair she cannot speak and when she started riding had to lie almost horizontally on a sheepskin, unable to straighten her legs. Five years later she has progressed to riding on a proper saddle, with stirrups, and with a little help can now hold herself upright while walking and trotting. Sharon is a perfect illustration of the misconception that most people have of the disabled. Because she has no control over her limbs and is unable to communicate through speech, it is easy to dismiss her as mentally handicapped. In fact she is a very bright woman who understands everything that is said and is very able with figures and computers. Thanks to her own indomitable spirit and to her mother Doris, she lead a very full life; she has a boyfriend and also a devoted helper in Colin, who brings Sharon and Doris to Wyvenhoe every week and walks alongside, giving a supporting hand when necessary, while Sharon rides. Her improvement has been remarkable and five years of riding have considerably strengthened her back muscles.

The physical exercise of riding has also helped Chris, a very cheerful young man who is known as Lester Piggott due to his unusual riding style – one leg jockey length, the other long. Spastic from birth he rode intermittently as a child until suffering a brain haemorrhage two years ago. Having recently returned to the saddle, riding is helping him to use his muscles again and at the same time giving him a great deal of enjoyment.

Di Cheveley, who now organises the Wednesday evening ride for adults, shows great pride in the achievements of 'her' riders while admitting to an understandable sadness that their state of health will never improve. A number have passed away, including Derek, who was paralysed on one side due to a severe stroke. Di recalls how one day, while threading the reins through the rigid fingers of his right hand, the instructor jokingly said, "You'll be the death of me." Derek's reply was a V-sign with his previously useless hand, a gesture which prompted his wife to take him back to the specialist who confirmed that riding had encouraged the return of movement to his fingers. Sadly his progress was halted by another stroke from which he did not recover.

The physical benefits of riding cannot be ignored. Unconsciously the handicapped learn to relax, to have fun and observe the countryside; to balance themselves and control the horse, and to become involved with what they are doing and what others are doing around them. But while riding is a form of therapy it is important that it is never regarded as a treatment. Its real value lies in the enjoyment the handicapped receive from an activity which makes them feel an accepted part of a community. This is sometimes lost on schools and residential centres which are home to many disabled people and decide who attends the weekly lessons. Mike is severely disabled and has shown little physical improvement since he started riding. However, group organiser Carry Kurk is determined that he will be allowed to continue. "He is part of our group," she says firmly, "although he does not communicate at all. Sometimes he make a dash to heaven knows where and is brought back chuckling to himself. Once on board a horse he smiles and then we know that he is enjoying himself. He doesn't hold on to the reins but somehow he still manages to stay on!"

Mike is sent by the Lockwood Day Centre whose riders currently range from the ages of 20 to 60. They suffer from a variety of disabilities including Downs Syndrome and epilepsy but most are severely mentally retarded with very little communication skills. Despite this, their Thursday morning ride is always full of fun and laughter.

"Sometimes we ride to music," explains Carry, "and if David recognises the music he can get quite vocal so he is known as 'Dave the Rave'. At Christmas we had a musical ride and invited all the parents and supporters to come and watch. David was in great form singing along to the carols. The whole show was masterminded by our instructor Keuke Kilmurry who has a wonderful understanding with her riders."

"The present Lockwood regulars have been coming for some time now," says Keuke. "Each in his or her own way is making progress and above all enjoying themselves. Tom is always smiling and talking and has almost succeeded in rising to the trot but much prefers jumping. Penny doesn't say much but makes sure we understand her enthusiasm in other ways, while Tracy finds the whole experience very daunting but once she is on board there is no stopping her.

"Michael is forever trying to run away from us but again, once he is mounted he does a mean rising trot and Jo, with the help of faithful and long suffering Blackie, puts many able bodied riders to shame. George had not ridden for a while after attempting to free-fall while dismounting a few months ago. However, he came to watch every week and is now steering Magic around the cones again."

Carry's Thursday ride also covers children from the Park School in Woking. Aged from eight to twelve the majority are slow learners or have Downs Syndrome but all enjoy their riding. There are no tantrums over which pony they will ride and the second ride wait patiently while their classmates have the first lesson. Lesha is eager for her turn and takes great delight in pointing out who is doing things wrong as the children have to perform a series of exercises in a certain order. "Riding is fun," she says. "I enjoy trotting best and I like riding Blackie."

Calvin is something of an enigma. He enjoys riding but hates to touch the pony and has to be lifted on. He always rides Pepper and at one time was adamant that he didn't want to ride any other pony. On one occasion he had to be duped into believing that the bay pony Star was in fact the palomino Pepper who had changed colour after rolling in the mud.

Calvin has to get used to riding different ponies if he is to go to summer camp and lifting him on to Jason produced surprisingly little objection on his part, much to the relief of Carry, and Rebecca who was instructing.

The children's confidence was obvious as they looked relaxed and happy. When an outburst of laughter among the spectators spooked one of the younger ponies his rider sat happily, totally unconcerned by the sudden movement. Lessons sometimes end with games and races which are always competitive. Although the competition may be fierce it is rarely negative as the riders all encourage each other.

"The children love cheering each other on," explains Carry, "and just love to win a rosette to take home. They actually do learn something during their lessons and if they are told the name of a part of the pony week after week they do sometimes start to remember."

For the physically handicapped riding provides s mobility which they prize above everything. Christine developed polio as a child and began riding at the age of 19. An accident four years ago when her horse bolted resulted in a broken leg and it was another year before she ventured back onto a horse. She still enjoys hacking but restricts her cantering to the indoor school. Supported by calipers and leg straps she rides with great confidence and also drives with the Stella Hancock Group.

"Riding is brilliant," she says. "It's great therapy and gives me a sense of freedom. When I am on a horse I'm on my own and I can get around whereas I can't when I'm on the ground. Driving is fun as well and I enjoy the social side of the shows and competitions but riding gives me more freedom."

"It is very difficult for me to say what I get out of horse riding," explains another woman for whom riding provides a welcome sense of independence. "I go once a week and I am lifted on to a horse; I then walk around for about half an hour before getting off. But there is much more to it than that. Just being able to use the words 'walk around' for someone who has spent all their life in a wheelchair is quite something. It means I can go over rough ground or up and down a step when I want to, just with a gentle pull on the reins. It means that instead of being just over four feet tall as I am in my wheelchair, I am over six feet tall and can see over hedges and fences instead of having to ask people what is on the other side, and so much more that it is difficult to put into words. I suppose just to say 'freedom' sounds rather glib but that is what riding means to me. To be able to move about where I want to without having to ask someone to give me a push."

Her words echo the statement made nearly 20 years ago by a reporter from a national newspaper after watching a ride of disabled children. "Lend those youngsters a pony's legs and, with a helping hand or two, they can forget their handicaps for a while and savour, even if subconsciously, the kind of mobility that should be their birthright but, through that one in a hundred chance, isn't."

Chapter Six
A Woman of Substance

Ben waits patiently by the mounting ramp in the indoor school, an air of quiet dignity on his large face. Mike lifts Pam into the saddle while Leslie, standing the other side of Ben, supports Pam with her hand. Legs are gently adjusted, feet placed in stirrups and reins organised. Once Pam is ready Ben walks forward on the lunge, Leslie chatting easily and asking Pam for her news of her mother and the exams which she took the previous week. The tension in Pam's body has nothing to do with fear or anxiety; having missed last week's lesson she is stiffer than usual. She asks Leslie if she can discard her stirrups for a whole; gradually the warmth from Ben's sides and the movement of his walking relax her muscles and slowly her legs begin to stretch downwards.

As she takes back her stirrups the difference in her leg position is illustrated by the way in which her feet now sit comfortably in the stirrups rather than reaching for them. In order to prevent herself from jogging Ben in the mouth Pam puts her right hand under the neck strap of his breastplate and pushes him into a trot. Sitting trot on a circle; Ben trots steadily almost shuffling his feet as he bends his legs – stiff as a result of advancing years – as little as possible. The slow trot jars Pam much less than a more lively action would and she offers the horse a stream of encouragement – "Good boy Ben, lovely Ben, my boy Ben."

Back to a walk and exercises encourage Pam to stretch her upper body. As she raises one arm above her head her balance is disturbed and she leans precariously to one side. Leslie tells Ben to stop and straightens Pam in the saddle before continuing. More sitting trot, right hand under the breastplate and the familiar encouragement – "lovely Ben, my boy Ben." Off the lunge and Pam steers Ben around the school while Leslie walks alongside correcting and praising in turn. As the lesson continues Pam's lower leg position becomes stronger and she sets off in trot on a solo circuit of the school. Her record is six laps at the trot but today she and Leslie call it a day after one.

Out in the sunshine Ben's reward is three peppermints which Pam produces from a wallet around her waist. Her lack of fear is not shared by Leslie, who admits to apprehension while Pam is riding and a worry that she will fall. "Pam has slipped before and fallen under the horse's legs," she explains. "But she is so enthusiastic and brave and I'm far more frightened of her falling than she is."

For Pam, the sensation of freedom and mobility, if only for half an hour a week, is clearly worth the risk. Her own riding is also helping Leslie's other disabled pupils. "Pam is very difficult to get on a horse at first," says Leslie, "and I have to gently pull her legs down. By the end of the lesson she's quite supple again. When I started to teach another boy with the same problem I was able to ask Pam for advice as I wasn't sure how far to push him. She was a great help to me as she can relate to others in the same position."

*   *   *

Pam Phillips is a remarkable woman. A victim of cerebral palsy, which results in a lack of communication between the brain and the body, she is the finest advertisement for a disabled person's right to live their life on equal terms with the able bodied. Lack of control over limbs and speech do not necessarily imply a lack of intelligence or understanding and her academic achievements are testament to her determination and ability. She is also a published author with a book of poems and donated the proceeds to the RDA. Now in her mid-forties she has been riding for nearly 20 years, having started through the West Horsley RDA group. Her involvement went beyond the weekly lessons and in 1977 she was given the opportunity to put forward the disabled person's point of view as the first disabled member of the group's committee.

Her steely determination to walk with sticks rather than accept a wheelchair is typical of Pam's tenacity and fighting spirit. Never one to accept fools gladly or to allow herself to be patronised, she care for her 85 year old mother in their Guildford home – shopping, cooking and cleaning. Currently studying for a history degree at Kingston Polytechnic, she explains the important part that riding has played, and continues to play in her life.

"My mother is terrified of horses but I get my love of riding from my father, whose family were farming people. He could ride before he could walk but I didn't start until I was 29. My parents couldn't afford riding lessons for me when I was young and so I didn't bother them about it, but I always liked horses and was only three when I first sat on one. We lived on a farm in Brecon and had a horse and plough as there were no tractors in those days. I used to go round all the animals, patting the cows, and the chickens used to come and sit on my lap.

"I always remember the first time I rode with the RDA. I was very excited and we went for a walk along the bridle path from Wyvenhoe. As a member of the West Horsley I passed all my RDA tests and went on to become the first person in the country to pass the RDA

Horsemasters. Part of the exam involved following the progress of a young dressage horse in training with Sarah Dwyer. I watched him working at home and in competition and wrote regular reports on his performance. It was very interesting and I found that an understanding of dressage improved my own riding. I know now where I am going wrong although I can't always put it right.

"I once finished fifth in an RDA dressage competition at Hever Castle on an old mare of June Childs' called Colleen. The previous day I went for a lesson and she wouldn't do anything I asked her. I was dreading the competition and rang Stella (Hancock) and told her, 'That Colleen's a stubborn old bugger; I couldn't do a thing with her today.' Stella just said, 'Don't worry Pam, just come along tomorrow and enjoy yourself.' The next day, when we got to the arena Colleen pricked up her ears and went marvellously. I do regret that I haven't found an outlet for all the work I did for my Horsemasters. I did try to become a dressage judge but was told that I'd never be accepted because I speak so slowly.

"I left the RDA in 1984 because it was felt that I could progress further if I rode privately. I joined an ordinary riding club which gave me confidence and now I have a lesson every week with Leslie Campbell at Wyvenhoe. If I get a bit down or depressed I get on a horse and feel good again. I don't know why. I tell Leslie that a good ride sets me up for the rest of the week, mentally and physically.

"Riding is not simply a matter of sitting on a horse and being led around a paddock. I am always trying to sit straight, upright position and use my legs to control the horse. My right hand does not relax and problems arise for me when I have to push my legs into the horse's sides to urge him on, as when I do this I automatically grip the reins tightly so the horse is in a dilemma and doesn't know whether to stop or go faster. One of the problems of cerebral palsy is that, as you get older, your legs become stiffer, and riding helps me because I have to move my legs. Often I wish they could be stretched. In the past I have ridden in a Western saddle which gave me more support but I think it is important to try and ride as properly as possible.

"Balance is the main key to riding and I do exercises with Leslie to improve my balance. Exercises sound tedious and reminiscent of my old days of physiotherapy but exercises on horseback present a challenge. When I am riding around the indoor school with one arm in the air I feel like someone riding a bicycle who is so confident they can ride without holding on to the handle bars.

"I never get frustrated riding because Leslie always encourages me and so I never feel that I can't do it. I get home sometimes and feel that I didn't work hard enough but Leslie says that when we spend time talking during a lesson I relax and that helps my riding. If I manage one or two good trots in a lesson then I feel that I have achieved something. I would like to be able to canter one day and get a reasonable mark in a dressage competition. Riding has helped me tremendously and given me the confidence to walk and swim. Some disabled people are encouraged to talk through their contact with animals, but lack of conversation has never been my impediment."

Chapter Seven
Beech Nut and Friends

When watching a group of disabled riders, while marvelling at their courage and determination it is easy to forget the importance of the animal underneath them. Horses and ponies used by the RDA must be quiet, obedient and totally reliable, able to cope with a rider being heaved on to their back, sudden movements and noises, and to remain totally unaffected by any commotion around them.

The early rides given by the West Horsley group relied on privately owned ponies from local families whose able bodied children became willing guinea pigs as they climbed all over the ponies and flopped about in the saddle to accustom the animals to riders with very little balance or coordination. "We had a trial at Hillside," recalls Kath Stevens, "to see if the ponies would put up with children being lifted on and taken off, the odd kick in the side, helpers all around them and the usual run of things that might happen."

Beech Nut, the original pony, had already proved his suitability and another Hancock pony, Dimple, also proved an ideal conveyance despite his rather unfortunate halitosis. They were joined by Kath Stevens' Conker, together with Merrylegs, Miner, Nutkin and Cobweb who were brought by their owners Sue Parker, Carol Riley, Jean Bishop and Chris Isaac – all stalwarts of the group whose hard work was vital to the development of the rides.

Finding suitable mounts was not always an easy task. Chris Isaac brought her son Stephen's second pony Riley to the lessons but after several weeks he developed a habit of bucking which made him unsafe for the young disabled pupils and they were unable to use him again. Others which were thought to be ideal proved a total disaster. Dennis and Prue Goodchild's solid, dependable cob was tried but did not like a rider being heaved up and then landing heavily in the saddle, so was rejected. Alternatively, some which at first glance would have been considered unlikely candidates proved to have perfect temperaments. Helen Turk recalls a five year old Grade B showjumper which had to be hastily enrolled when a lame pony caused a shortage. Although inexperienced with beginners he looked after his handicapped riders and didn't put a foot wrong.

With the move to Wyvenhoe in 1973 Beech Nut and friends were replaced by the riding school horses and ponies and the pupils had to learn some different names – Sinbad, Colleen, Sonny, Shadow, Gypsy, Punch, Amber and Napoleon. Although used to beginners some of the Wyvenhoe animals proved unsuitable as they reacted nervously to wheelchairs and the special mounting ramps used for the disabled. Generally, however, the calibre of the horses was very high and the regulars were rewarded after a number of years with long service medals which they wore on their bridles.

One or two of the horses used when the group first moved to Wyvenhoe have only recently retired. One-eyed Sinbad, at the grand age of 34, was given an emotional send off in the indoor school by pupils from the Park School. After a lap of honour wearing a red sash, he was given a goodbye gift of a hamper filled with apples, carrots, horse biscuits and peppermints, which was gratefully received by Leslie Campbell.

Many tears were shed over Sinbad's retirement as he was much loved by all, including one of the Thursday helpers. "Having joined the West Horsley as a helper in 1977 I was given several ponies to lead but after a year or so I seemed to be teamed with Sinbad quite often. A pony of real character, with only one eye due to an accident in his youth, we got on very well together. This was probably because I always carried some Polo mints for him in my pocket.

"Gradually I began to understand his ways. He didn't believe in the theory that if the rider was disabled then the pony should always be willing. If he was unhappy with his rider he would let me know in no uncertain terms, trying to push me off the track and generally being as awkward as possible."

The affection with which the disabled children in particular regard the ponies was illustrated by one six year old boy who refused to ride or speak by would spend hours sitting in a stable talking to the pony.

Two weeks after Sinbad's retirement, Ben, a mere youngster of 32, also bid farewell to his working days which, like Sinbad's had been confined in recent years to RDA duties. With retirement, however, comes the problem of what to do with a 30 year old animal that has led an active life. Leisurely days in a field may sound like a perfect solution but often results in crippling laminitis, and limbs used to stretching and working every day soon become stiff and painful with inactivity.

It is difficult not to feel that the majority would be more suited by continuing in semi-retirement with the light, undemanding work of RDA lessons to keep them relatively fit and active. The decision is usually out of the hands of the riding school but instead is the responsibility of the veterinary officer appointed by the council, who regularly visits riding schools to check on the welfare of the horses. Sometimes, however, rather than improving a horse's life retirement leads to a degeneration in condition which results in the animal having to be put down. The health and fitness of the animals is always of paramount importance to the RDA and no horse or pony is subjected to any form of abuse, such as constant jabs in the mouth or a heavy rider bumping up and down in the saddle, while being used by the handicapped. The riders themselves are not allowed to show any sign of temper and any tantrums can result in the end of the lesson for that rider.

The phasing out of many of the most reliable animals at Wyvenhoe is now presenting the group with another problem, as Leslie Legg explains. "When the RDA first started here we had a group of dependable horses and ponies and we've worked with them for 20 years. Now of course we've got a lot in their thirties so it's years since we've had to bring new horses in and we're finding it very difficult even to find animals for the riding school. You forget how cheeky young ponies can be but we do find that the routine of daily lessons settles them down and then we gradually filter the ones we can trust into RDA work." With many of the riding school stables now occupied by liveries there are also fewer horses available as livery owners generally are not willing to let their horses be used by the riding school or the RDA.

Thoroughbreds are never used for handicapped riders but otherwise there is no breed discrimination and even arabs have proved suitable for those with less severe handicaps. It is not merely a quiet horse that is required; it must be patient, reliable and unflappable. The mentally handicapped, in particular, are sometimes very noisy and those animals unnerved by strange sounds emitted by the rider cannot be used safely with the very handicapped.

The most remarkable aspect of riding with disabled people is the horses' apparent understanding of their vulnerability and the sense of responsibility which this seems to produce. "The horses at Wyvenhoe are amazing," says Di Cheveley. "When I go to tack them up on a cold winter's evening most of them have already done a full day's work and really don't want to go out again. They are as unhelpful as possible while I get them ready but as soon as they get into the indoor school with the disabled they behave perfectly. They seem to know that these riders need a little more care taken of them."

In order to provide reliable animals for the handicapped the RDA has a system of testing privately owned ponies to judge their suitability. On one memorable occasion during a show at Ardingly in Sussex the testing of RDA ponies – which involved a good deal of noise and commotion – resulted in the involuntary dismount of most of the competitors in the next door ridden hunter class. Sarah Garnett is involved in the testing of ponies and admits that it can be a very difficult task. "Some people feel that you have no right to criticise their animals when they are prepared to let them be used. I went to test one pony whose owner was very keen for it to be used by the RDA but its temperament was completely wrong. It made horrible faces and twice tried to bite me and I had to point out to the lady owner that, to a person in a wheelchair unable to move out of the way, that would be very worrying. She was furious, however, that I wouldn't accept the pony. We really do have to be quite thick skinned sometimes and not get upset by people. One thing I have learned is that you can criticise a woman's children, or even seduce her husband, but you must never criticise her horse."

The most famous RDA pony is of course Rags, who was bought with funds raised by the BBC television programme Blue Peter, but the West Horsley had its own Rags in Rotary Albert, a ride and drive Fell type pony bought for the group with money donated by the local Rotary Club. Unfortunately Albert did not prove suitable and had to be sold.

A number of horses are donated to the RDA but these are often unsuitable and the association now has a welfare department to deal with the problem. Children often become fond of a particular pony and this can sometimes result in tears if two or three of them want to ride the same pony or the animal is unavailable. For this reason the riders are swapped around as much as possible, although some might be kept on a particular horse whenever possible to increase their confidence. This confidence gained from an undemanding animal will often open up a new world to a disabled person and transform their life. It is a debt which the horses and ponies never ask to be repaid.

Chapter Eight
Tina's First Ride

In October 1993 the Wednesday evening ride of the Horsley RDA group took on a new rider. Thirty two year old Tina had been born with no eyes and was about to discover the thrill of riding on an animal she had never seen and could not even visualise. Group organiser Diana Cheveley describes Tina's first steps into a new world.

*   *   *

"It was on a bitterly cold, late October evening that Tina came for her first ride with us. The Royal School for the Blind had provided us with the essential information we need to prepare for new riders, namely height, weight, disability and any personality disorders. In Tina's case we were told she was born without eyes and was very nervous of animals but keen to learn to ride. Armed with these facts we knew we would have to proceed very slowly with her and get her used to being near a horse before we even thought of putting her on one.

"Aaron, a lovely chestnut gelding with four white socks, was chosen for his temperament and ability to carry Tina's height and weight. Once tacked up, with the added safety measures of neck strap and leading rein held firmly by our helper Amanda, we introduced him to Tina in a quiet corner of the indoor school. Rosemary and I gently invited Tina to stroke Aaron's nose and placed her woolly, gloved hand on the soft pink tip between his nostrils.

"He did not move a muscle and after a few minutes, as Tina couldn't feel his whiskers, we suggested she remove her glove, which she duly did. This took more courage as she could then feel the soft breath on her skin and Aaron's whiskers tickling her hand. We then began to guide Tina's hand up along the full length of Aaron's face, feeling his forelock and his long ears. She seemed surprised at the size of his head and continued to stroke him, gently brushing her hand over his eye, through his thick golden mane and down his furry neck. Still Aaron stood motionless.

"The voyage of discovery continued down one front leg to his white sock and then along his back, taking in the saddle which she would sit in – feeling its depth and shape – and down the leather to the stirrup in which she would place her foot. Only occasionally did Tina momentarily withdraw her hand as she explored. Then she would take a deep breath and say to herself, 'You can do it', before continuing.

"Had Aaron twitched his head or fidgeted Tina would undoubtedly have recoiled, but he stood like a rock, only his eyes blinking, as if he knew the importance of his task. Tina's confidence was growing. She now had an impression of Aaron's shape and when I asked if she felt like sitting in the saddle, to our surprise she readily consented.

"The next step was to secure the chin-strap on her hat and put a double handled belt around her waist. We than explained the intricacies of the mounting block and how Amanda would lead Aaron to stand alongside it. Tina would now find that instead of reaching up to Aaron's back and the saddle, she would be on a higher level and able to climb on to his back more easily.

"Rosemary and I carefully led Tina to the mounting block and placed one of her hands on the rail. Holding on to me with the other hand, she counted with me up the four wide steps to the top of the platform and turned towards the pony. Seeing that we were ready, Amanda guided Aaron alongside, where he stopped and awaited his passenger.

"Gripping the saddle, Tina let us put her left foot into the stirrup and guide her right leg over the horse's back and before she knew it, she was astride. She sat for a few moments in disbelief, inhaling deeply and verbally encouraging herself. We placed the other foot in the stirrup, put the reins into her hands – still with one glove on and one off – and curled her fingers around the pommel. Tina told us that she remembered riding a rocking horse as a child and wondered whether the motion would be the same when the pony moved off. Sitting tall in the saddle and taking one more deep breath, she was ready to find out.

"Off we set to join on behind the rest of the ride. Denise, our instructor, came over to welcome Tina and introduce herself, telling her simply to relax and accustom herself to the movement. "As horses have four legs you will be able to count the four beats as he walks along," Denise announced. Tina was enthralled – 'one, two, three, four', she repeated as Aaron walked around the school. 'I can really feel the beats.'

"Before long Tina had learned that by pulling gently back on the reins Aaron would stop and then by squeezing with her legs and saying 'Walk on Aaron' she could make the pony respond to her commands. Her smile broadened by the moment as she repeated the process over and over again.

"This was enough for Tina's first ride, which had been quite exhilarating. Amanda led Aaron back to the mounting-block where once again he stood motionless as Tina listened carefully to our instructions on how to dismount. With both feet out of the stirrups, Tina easily found the mounting block with her left foot so, leaning forward, Rosemary guided her other leg over Aaron's back and I then guided it to the mounting-block.

"With Tina holding on to the rail with one hand and me with the other we counted the steps down to the floor, where Tina happily patted Aaron and thanked him for looking after her. We said our farewells and assured Tina that Aaron, Amanda, Rosemary and I would be waiting for her the following week.

"I put Aaron's rug over his back and, with ears pricked and contentedly munching on Polos, he was led back to his stable by Amanda. He had been a star and I think he knew it!"

Chapter Nine
A Helping Hand

Possibly the hardest job with an RDA group is that of helpers organiser. For every class there has to be three helpers available for each rider – one to lead the pony while the other two walk either side of the rider, ready to lend a helping hand if necessary. As the riders progress some are able to ride unaided or with only one helper to lead the pony but nevertheless every group is dependent on the band of willing volunteers who turn up every week to help ensure that the disabled riders are never disappointed.

Carol Riley, who compiled a list of 50 volunteers when she was appointed the first helpers organiser in 1970, recalls: "There was always a handful of helpers that you knew would never let you down and the rest you had to bully and ring them up to say, 'Are you coming?' Even so we always somehow managed to have enough people." Sybil Atherton, who took over as helpers organiser in 1975, found that she was often left with a last minute search for helpers as some cancelled on the morning of the ride. "There were some very ingenious excuses, along with the usual doctors and dentists appointments, and funerals were always on a Tuesday! The best helpers are those that always turn up on time."

"It is not essential for helpers to have any extensive knowledge of riding and horses," Stella Hancock always insisted, "but it is vital that they should feel some duty – enjoyable hopefully – to turn up regularly, on time, ready to help in any way they can, even if it is only to walk beside the rider as a support. In short, there is a job for anyone whose heart is in it."

An official description of the helpers' role states: 'The prime function of the person leading the pony is to control it under all circumstances. To keep a good distance from the other ponies and to make sure it moves at a comfortable pace and stands properly during the exercises. To be alert to the orders of the person taking the ride. The prime function of the helpers on either side of the rider is his, or her, safety and comfort. To help the rider relax and be happy, and at all times to be alert to the rider's needs. To be alert to the instructions of the person taking the ride and to anticipate the rider's reactions and capabilities.'

No willing volunteer is ever turned away. Those unfamiliar with horses soon become aware of the need to refrain from sudden movements and loud noises and, while a fear of horses can be a problem, the most vital requirements are patience, good humour and an ability to communicate. The limited time available for each ride means that quick changeovers are vital. The same ponies are usually used but different tack is sometimes required and helpers need to be aware of any necessary alterations and be able to carry them out with the minimum of fuss.

Helpers come in all shapes and sizes and occasionally in surprising packages. A girl who turned up one evening with green and orange hair, rings all over her ears and nose and dressed in weird and wonderful clothes which it was feared would scare the horses, proved to be brilliant with both the animals and the riders. Minutes of an early committee meeting include the note: 'Mrs Hancock reported that Mrs Crampton of the Red Cross had offered to help with anything that was not actually connected with the ponies.' Volunteers are not only required for the lessons; providing refreshments is an important task and coffee ladies such as Mimi Widney, who gave six years of service, are a vital part of the group. "Mimi was a stickler for good order," recalls Ron Hancock. "She presided over the coffee with a firm hand and would never allow anyone to have a drink unless they had earned it. But she always had a big smile and was a great encouragement to everyone."

The reasons for becoming involved with the RDA vary. Some are grateful for healthy children and grandchildren and, having spent their lives with horses and ponies, are eager to help those not so fortunate. Others have a handicapped child or relation, although many with family problems find the contact with other handicapped children too traumatic and close to home. A number of adults who come to help find it too upsetting; some find communication with the mentally handicapped difficult and soon give up, while others are not prepared to commit themselves to a morning or afternoon every week. With any organisation in need of volunteers there are always plenty of people who show initial enthusiasm, but the percentage of those who follow it through is usually fairly low. A stand at the local Surrey County Show during the 1970s elicited an interested response from the general public in the work of the West Horsley but out of every 25 people who volunteered help, perhaps only one would become a regular.

Helpers play a vital role in assisting the instructor to communicate with the riders and so must concentrate on the lesson to enable them to fulfil their role. Constant chattering with each other not only makes the instructor's job more difficult but also confuses the riders, most of whom can only concentrate on one voice at a time. "Some helpers used to chatter constantly to each other," says June Childs. "This made it very difficult to teach the children and means that they are not looking after the children properly."

Helen Turk agrees that a good helper is very important and can be a great asset to the instructor. "An incommunicative child could be encouraged to speak by telling them to ask the pony to 'walk on'. If the child managed to say something, the helper if they were concentrating could quietly nudge the pony to make it walk on, so the child would think the pony had responded to their command and would feel encouraged to talk to the pony again." While the occasional helping hand can be beneficial, however, helpers are generally asked to let their disabled charges do as much as possible for themselves. A good helper has to create a balance between encouragement and domination.

The RDA is one of the few organisations in which a great many people become physically involved and helpers need to be reasonably fit and agile in order to keep up with the horses. Riders who need to be supported in the saddle can easily be unbalanced by a helper hanging on to their clothing or special belt as they struggle to keep up. Suitable footwear designed for running is important and open-toed sandals are likely to prove vulnerable to a well placed, iron shod hoof. The effort required in lifting a disabled person on to a horse makes it difficult to cope with heavier adults and has necessitated a weight limit for riders of eleven stone.

Men are always valued as helpers – their physical strength often proving invaluable. Husbands are often enrolled, such as John Parker, whose task it was to collect the jumps for the annual show. "They were the local Pony Club jumps," he recalls, "and had always 'just been repainted' so we had to be very careful not to knock them against each other. They were the pride and joy of a lady called Una Mizen who was one of the greats of the Cranleigh Group, and we were frightened to death of her."

Contact with the disabled brings the realisation that they do not need to be patronised or humoured. Di Cheveley recalls her first experience as a helper, back in 1976. "I was supposed to look after a five year old girl with Downs Syndrome and chattered inanely away to her as I tacked up the pony. She glowered at me until finally, in response to my comment, 'Doesn't Dumpling look smart', she said firmly, 'I don't want to ride that f...ing pony and I don't want you, I want the lady with brown hair.' It certainly took me by surprise but it was the last time I tried to humour a disabled child."

In many cases helpers receive just as much benefit from their involvement as the riders. Some get a great deal of enjoyment from the contact with the animals and find it very rewarding to watch the riders improve and master new accomplishments. As one helper commented, "The RDA has taught me to treat the disabled as normal people. Before, I never really knew how to talk to someone with a disabled child – it was almost like a bereavement in the family." One devoted helper who had ridden as a child rediscovered riding as a result of her experience with the West Horsley. Having reached the age of 70 she had to retire as a helper but, her enthusiasm rekindled by her regular contact with the horses at Wyvenhoe, she began to ride again and is now jumping and enjoying every moment.

The encouragement of the helpers draws the mentally handicapped out of their shells and many of the children become very attached to a particular helper. This can cause a problem if the helper is absent for any reason and, as with the ponies, an effort is made to mix riders and helpers as much as possible.

Regular contact with the severely handicapped could perhaps induce feelings of sadness or frustration but the happiness and fun involved with riding produces an opposite reaction. Sybil Atherton explains: "The riders were enjoying themselves and having fun, so you never felt sorry for them. We never saw the sadder side of their lives and didn't spend enough time with them to become emotionally involved. I used to get lovely letters from some of the mothers, thanking me for doing so much for their children, and it always seemed a very worthwhile thing to do."

It is difficult to mention all the many wonderful helpers the Group has had over the years and their tremendous loyalty, but one such person is Sonia Windsor, who was there when the Group started with Paul Creswell in 1961 and is still doing so much to help more than 25 years later. It is quite amazing how many of the Group's so called "Golden Oldies" are still giving such valuable help. Were it not for the helpers, there wouldn't be a story to tell.

Chapter Ten
Riding to Remission

At the age of 36, Surrey housewife Clare Cox was struck down with multiple sclerosis which affects the spine and can result in paralysis. The symptoms of this devastating illness appeared after a bout of 'flu and her condition gradually deteriorated, rendering her weaker and less mobile by the day. Offered little hope of recovery by her doctor, Clare turned to riding as a way of exercising. Her remarkable story is a tribute to her own determination and another example of the therapeutic bond between man and horse.

* * *

"I appeared to develop multiple sclerosis almost overnight. I had 'flu and one minute I was fine and the next I got out of bed and fell over. I didn't walk properly again for seven years; my condition became gradually worse and at its peak I had very little movement. The doctors said that I simply had to wait and see if I got better or worse but I just thought 'rubbish'. So I kissed goodbye to the medical profession and did what I felt I could do at any given time.

"I'd been disabled for about six months and was walking very badly on two sticks. One day I was watching our youngest son Jeremy riding his new pony around the yard and I thought that would be a good thing for me to try. I had ridden a lot as a child but not for about 20 years. When I got on the pony I was absolutely terrified although there were two people holding me on. The pony was absolutely marvellous. I could hardly hold the reins but as I rode her quietly around the yard with my feet hanging loose I could feel the strength oozing back into my spine.

"That was the start and I made sure that I did it every day, no matter how ghastly I was feeling. Sometimes I really enjoyed it and at other times it was purgatory but I never did more than walk. Occasionally I'd do exercises, such as stretching up and flopping down and twisting from side to side; sometimes I'd ride with my feet in the stirrups. On bad days I'd only ride for a few minutes but on good days I'd ride fairly normally and you wouldn't have known there was anything wrong with me. I always felt stronger afterwards although the effect would last for anything from half an hour to the rest of the day.

"Jeremy's pony was only 12.2 hands and very forward going with a fast walk and I noticed that when I rode a friend's quiet old horse the effect was not the same. On a slow, plodding horse where I had to use my legs I simply got very tired. It wasn't using my legs that was so beneficial, it was sitting on a forward going animal and absorbing the movement. I think that for anyone with very weak legs, smaller, quicker moving ponies are better. However, when you are at your weakest your immediate reaction is to hang on for dear life and a very forward going pony can be quite frightening. So it is important to have plenty of sympathetic helpers around to hold you on if necessary and encourage you to relax.

"It is not merely the physical sensation, however; the mental stimulus is also very important. You have to think about what you are doing when you ride and there is I think something almost spiritual between man and horse. If you are tense or worried that feeling soon disappears if you go and spend a little time with a horse. The old saying that there is something about the outside of a horse that is so good for the inside of a man is very true. One can't say that the physical benefits are greater than the mental effect, as one generally follows the other. On a day when I was feeling frustrated by my own physical shortcomings, the physical sensation gave me the biggest lift, but when I was feeling depressed riding made me feel psychologically better as I felt I'd achieved something just by sitting on the pony.

"I was very lucky because I had access to a pony and friends who were willing to help me so I was able to ride every day and didn't need to join an RDA group. Whether riding helped me because I had ridden before I don't know, but I do feel it is well worth any disabled person joining an active RDA group where there are plenty of helpers to instil confidence. It was also easier for me because I had people who I trusted to help me rather than strangers and I was allowed to go at my own pace. It is important to remember that the disabled don't always want to *do* something when they are riding. Quite often they just want the opportunity to sit on a pony and be aware of their body obtaining strength. Instructors and helpers need to have a great deal of patience and understanding and be prepared to go at the disabled person's pace and not their own. There can be a tendency to want riders to progress but they don't need to in that sense. It is progress enough for many disabled just to sit on a moving animal and experience the freedom that it provides. Not everyone wants to learn to trot once they have walked.

"Seven years after I developed multiple sclerosis I gradually began to feel stronger and since then I have been in remission. I am now more or less back to normal although I do get tired. I still ride and find that I can ride perfectly adequately unaided at walk, trot and canter. The pony we have now is 14.2 hands and a bit slower than our 12.2. Sometimes I have to work quite hard but I have reached the stage where it helps me to use my legs as it makes them stronger. If I am feeling grotty I always feel better if I go out for a ride.

"As I was so much better I felt that the least I could do is to help others not so fortunate and, through a friend, I joined the Stella Hancock Driving Group as a helper. When I first went along to a session my immediate reaction was to run away and then I wanted to cry. Then I thought, 'That's not going to help anybody, but if I hold a pony or put someone's hat on, that is being useful.'

"I was fortunate because I have a very supportive family and they wouldn't let me become an invalid. I don't think my remission has happened because of my determination to get better but I did try to help myself by not giving up. I certainly made myself worse on some days by thrashing myself into some sort of normal existence and there were days when I felt better if I simply relaxed. You really have to listen to your body and do as much as you feel you can do at the time.

"I don't know how long my remission will last but every day is precious. When I first started to deteriorate I was very frightened because nothing I did seemed to help. The only therapy that did seem to make a difference was riding the pony and the physiotherapist I was working with is convinced that it was riding that kept me out of a wheelchair."

Chapter Eleven
Summer Holidays

While RDA groups are able to provide handicapped children with weekly rides during the term time, school holidays for many are not the weeks of freedom and activity enjoyed by other children. To some parents a handicapped child is a source of shame and embarrassment, to others merely an inconvenience. The Park School at Woking has a number of pupils who, though physically able bodied, have learning difficulties for one reason or another. Their home life is sometimes unhappy, which often contributes to their behavioural problems, and the concept of a holiday is something they have never experienced.

Holiday schemes for the disabled are available but expensive. With this in mined Yvonne Fisk, who had become involved with the West Horsley as a helper, conceived the idea of a summer camp for the Park School children, run on similar lines to a Pony Club camp. A newly constructed stable block at her idyllic home near Guildford provided accommodation for three ponies, a tack room and a barn, which was converted into two dormitories for the campers.

The first camp was held in 1981 and organised by Yvonne Fisk and Helen Turk and six children chosen by the school arrived for their three day holiday. Park School, anxious because many of the pupils had never spent the night away from home, requested a chaperone to stay with the children at night – a responsibility that Yvonne took on personally. She was equally apprehensive as it was unknown territory for everyone and quite an undertaking to keep six hyperactive children occupied for three days. All the fears proved groundless, however, and the camp was an immediate success. As a result Yvonne decided to run the camp over six days the following year, to allow them to entertain two groups of six children for three days each.

Since then it has flourished and become an annual highlight, offering children in some cases the only holiday they will ever have. The campers are all aged between 10 and 13 and chosen by Park School from the pupils who ride on Thursday afternoons and are considered most in need of a holiday. Some attend two or three times and might include a 14 year old who the school feels is desperately in need of a break. Whenever possible three boys and three girls are sent to provide a balance but there is provision for four and two as one dormitory is big enough for four beds.

When the children arrive on the first morning they have a short riding lesson to give Yvonne an idea of their capabilities, but for the next three days fun is the operative word and the children enjoy games and long hacks through the surrounding fields and woods. With more time to ride than the usual half hour, they progress noticeably, some even learning to canter.

The ponies are all borrowed from neighbours and friends and are usually more forward going than those at Wyvenhoe. Even so, in 13 years only three children have been unseated which is a tribute to Yvonne's organisation and her determination not to treat the campers with kid gloves. She recalls how one pony, Burgundy, had trouble keeping up at the trot and would break into canter, sometimes putting in the odd buck. A couple of the children were caught out but were soon back on board, none the worse for their fall. Another pony with the wonderful name of Abandon Hope is very good with children but has been known to bolt so is never let off the leading rein.

While the camp ponies might show more spirit that the average riding school mount Yvonne does insist that they are 100% reliable in the stable. "We try to treat the children as perfectly normal," she explains, "and not worry about them any more than you would about any child with a pony. Some lack coordination and are highly strung which makes them tense, but at camp they are probably more relaxed than at any other time because they are enjoying themselves. While they are here they help to get the ponies tacked up and look after them, something they don't do at Wyvenhoe, so the ponies must be totally reliable in the stable. The ponies are essential as they provide the excuse to run the camp, but the biggest asset of the three days is that the children are having a holiday. They are having fun and spending time with people who are there to entertain them and make sure they enjoy themselves. They would never sit down quietly and read a book; they always want to be doing something energetic so it is very tiring but the children get so much out of it."

The amount of running around involved by the helpers makes it a more suitable task for the younger generation and almost without exception the campers respond to the company of helpers their own age who are willing to play endless games of rounders, football and so on. It is not merely the physical aspect that prompts Yvonne to enrol younger troops. "I couldn't run this camp with people my age," she says, "because they would be too bossy and the children would have to behave themselves too well all the time. They are here to have fun."

A number of the helpers who generally range in age from 13 to 23, use the week to work towards their Duke of Edinburgh's gold or silver award, for which Yvonne's camp provides more than the necessary 40 hours of residential experience with the disabled. Some campers also return as helpers. "There is one boy", says Yvonne, "who has now left Park School but returned here last year as a helper and is coming again this summer. He is pretty impossible and worse than the children sometimes because five minutes after he's started something he forgets what he's meant to be doing – he has no retentive ability at all. But he is always bright, clean and very polite. His mother left home and the father now looks after four sons, one of which is in a home and the other three have all been at Park School. He is a delightful man and has obviously brought them up very well but, by some genetic coincidence, all the boys are slow learners."

Although problems are often caused by nature rather than neglect Yvonne feels strongly that many children are handicapped by their upbringing. "So many of them are deprived," she explains. "They say things like 'Can I have a whole tomato miss?' and they've never seen strawberries and other things that we take for granted. To see their faces tucking into strawberries, ice cream and chocolate sauce is wonderful."

Yvonne recalls one little girl who arrived for camp with her clothes in such a terrible state of repair that they had to find others to fit her. When her parents arrived at the end of camp they came in an expensive car, accompanied by their beautifully dressed elder daughter on whom they had obviously lavished everything they felt would have been wasted on their handicapped child.

While riding is the main activity during camp the action is non-stop throughout the three days with swimming, barbecues, treasure hunts, visits to the milking parlour on the local farm and to Thorpe Park, where they receive free tickets and the children can enjoy all the exciting rides. One of the most enjoyable outings is to Helen Turk's home at nearby Cobham, where she and her husband heat and floodlight their swimming pool for their special guests and supper is provided in the form of fish and chips.

Card games are also popular and many of the children show an unexpected talent for card playing, together with a 'streetwise' grasp of the value of money. Rain can often dampen any occasion but seldom manages to lower the spirits of the campers. One heavy storm resulted in a flood and the unusual attire of shorts and wellies but Yvonne is able to cope with drenched clothes and children with the minimum of fuss and cannot remember a time when everyone was forced indoors by the vagaries of the English weather.

Bedtime is often after 11 o'clock, accompanied by hot chocolate. Yvonne now leaves the responsibility of night-time chaperone to one of the younger helpers and there are few problems. All the children are sent with any relevant medical notes and most eventualities are covered.

An army marches on its stomach and food is plentiful and nourishing as everyone is always hungry. Chicken, sausages, beefburgers and jacket potatoes are the mainstays.

Breakfast is cooked in the tack room but the other meals are organised from Yvonne's farmhouse kitchen with military precision. Feeding campers and helpers forms a large part of the cost of camp, which amounts to around £700. Fund raising varies from the sale of books and badges to collecting tins at local pubs and saddlers. Other schemes have included rides in a trap with 'Father Christmas' and for many years the camp was sponsored by a runner in the London Marathon. Help has come from the local Rotary Club and a number of local businesses provide goods either free of charge or at a special rate.

Inevitably over the years there has been the odd hiccup at camp but never a total disaster. In the early days the walls of the dormitories were constructed from bales of hay which affected a number of the children who suffered from asthma. The hay was then replaced by two scaffolding poles and 'curtains' of old bedspreads which are often knocked over but don't result in coughing and wheezing.

Camp ends with a gymkhana to which the parents are invited. Not all bother to attend even though the school offers to collect those without transport. Rosettes are awarded and all the children manage to win their share to take home. Just to ensure that no-one goes home empty-handed, Yvonne if necessary introduces 'Nobby's race' which all the helpers leading the ponies know must be won by the rider who has yet to win a rosette.

Before leaving, the children sign cards to everyone who has helped to make camp possible, and the variety of letters and drawings that Yvonne receives once they are back at school is more than enough to show just how much their three day holiday is appreciated. Some will return the following year. None of them will ever forget it.

Top: Leslie Nightingale (left) with John Murray on Beech Nut and Jan Farrant during the early days at Hillside Farm.
Bottom: Angela Duffin (left) with Betty riding Conker and Gilly Blake and Kath Stevens.

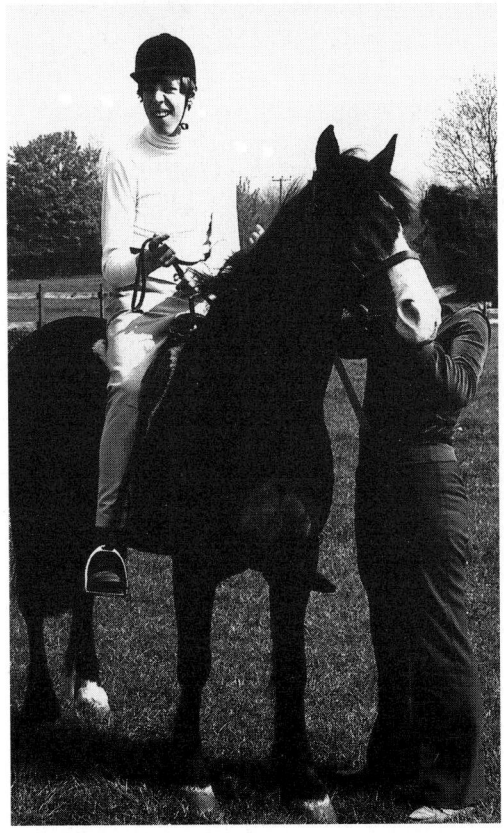

Above: Michael Kelly one of the spina bifida riders with Iva de Wilton, Patsie Waugh and Kath Stevens at Hever Castle. Michael was the winner of the dressage competition.

Left: Paul Creswell on Coleen. He was the first disabled rider at Hillside Farm in September 1968 and because of him a group was started at West Horsley to provide riding for other disabled children.

Right: A young rider from Templecourt representing the West Horsley group in a dressage competition at Arundel Castle.

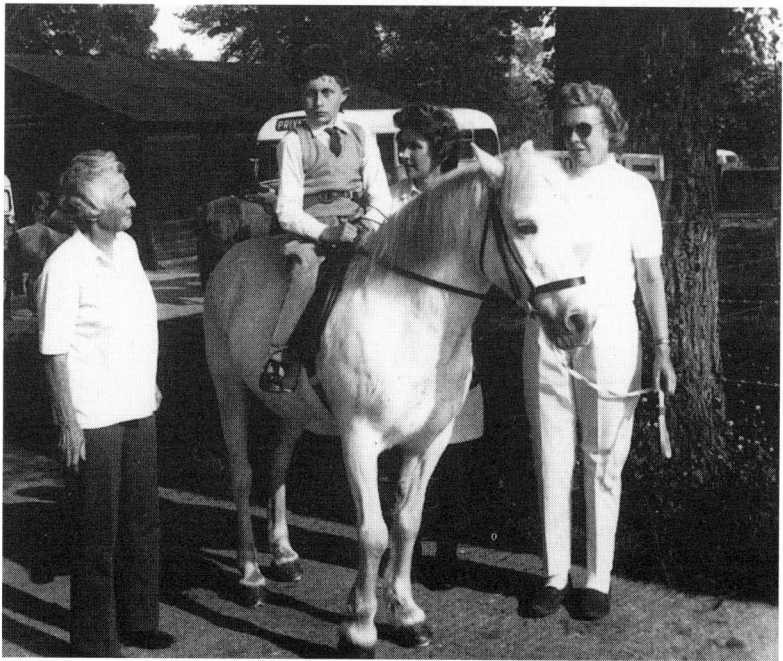

Above: Muriel Whittock (left) with Leslie Brown riding Merrylegs and Joan Crampton and Barbara Wilson during one of the early rides at Hillside Farm.

Left: Sarah Garnett (right) helping seven-year-old Samantha Gill to get ready for a competition at Goodwood, watched by her mother Janet and her sister Nikki.

Centre: the West Horsley driving group during their early days with the new Jubilee carts and the 'ace' cart designed by Jack Burrill.
Bottom: the Duchess of Norfolk assisted by the Area Chairman Tora Bray presenting a prize to Hassan, the dressage winner at Hever Castle.

Above: a happy group of riders and helpers with Gilly Blake (left), Jennifer Smith (centre) and Christine Isaac (right). The physiotherapist Patricia Rutter is in the background.

Right: Betty Holroyd leading Harry Fortune, a young spina bifida rider.

Above: Michele Hampson, a 22-year-old Down syndrome rider with the group.

Above: the dark bay pony Jason who was one of the most popular with the riders.

Above: Neil Portsmouth driving Prince accompanied by Valantine Cadell. Neil drives from his wheelchair and is now a keen member of the Driving Committee.

Right: One of the group's senior riders about to compete in a dressage test.

Below: Paula Stebbing with Michael Kelly at the Hever Castle area dressage competition. Michael was second at his first dressage competition, but was determined to win on this occasion and succeeded in doing so.

Top: HRH Princess Anne and Sue Parker, the group organiser (left), at the opening of the new tack room. Gordon Walker is on the right with Hugh Gemmell, the group's first blind rider.
Bottom: giving a word of encouragement to one of the youngest riders.

Above: Sheila Ingram driving Justin from her wheelchair at the RHA Barracks, accompanied by the pony's owner, Jack Burril.

Above: Anthony Kerslick at Hever Castle before the dressage test with Helen Turk (left) and Leslie Smith.

Left: Jo from the Lockwood Centre riding Blackie led by Anne with Keuke Kilmurry, her instructor, on the right.

Above: Vehicle builder Ken Jackson loading a wheelchair into one of his driving vehicles.

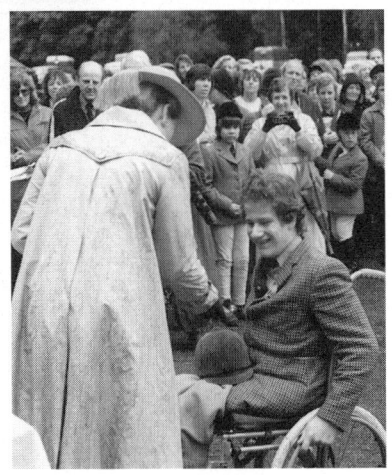

Above: HRH Princess Anne presenting a rosette to Michael Kelly, a popular member of the group.

Above: Gillian Cummings jumping on Sinbad with Diana Cheveley running alongside.

Above: HRH Prince Philip pinning a rosette to the bridle of Miss Muffet driven by Pam Le Motte accompanied by Valentine Cadell at the Windsor BDS Annual Show in 1985.

Above: Andrew Cowdery (in wheelchair) receiving a cheque for £2053.50 towards his Wheels Account watched by his father and Jill Holah (standing) and Mr and Mrs Tony Brand (seated in the vehicle). Andrew Cowdery, although not a member of the Horsley groups, is an experienced driver and works tirelessly for disabled driving.

Above: Frances Johns leading Coleen during the open day at Wyvenhoe in July 1982, watched by the pony, Gay.

Right: Helen Turk (left) and Prue Goodchild, two long-term stalwarts of the group, with one of the young riders.

Above: HRH Princess Anne (right) talking to Stella Hancock after an RDA Council meeting at the Saddler's Hall in London.

Above: a happy group of riders relaxing after one of the sessions at Wyvenhoe.

Right: Laura Hayward having a jumping lesson on Aaron at Wyvenhoe, accompanied by Emma.

Right: the skewbald pony Harley with one of the riders.

Right: Neil Portsmouth driving the coloured pony Pebbles at Smith's Lawn, Windsor, accompanied by Brenda May.

Top: Her Majesty the Queen talking to one of the officials at the BDS Show at Smith's Lawn.
Bottom: HRH Prince Philip with Col. Sir John Miller, President of the British Driving Society, and competitors in the RDA Fancy Dress Class. at Windsor.

The group was placed second in the Fancy Dress Class at the Royal Windsor Horse Show in 1980.
Right: several of the members dressed as circus clowns, including Paula Stebbing, Kath Stevens, Sonia Windsor and Tania Windsor with Anna Gale on the pony.
Centre: another enthusiastic group member.

Above: Renee on Pepper as Worzel Gummage with Diana Cheveley.
Right: an impressive scarecrow.

81

Above: Neil Portsmouth with Pauline Farino driving her pony, Bubbly, in the musical drive at the World Four in Hand Championships at Ascot in August 1986. Behind is Milly Millington driving Christopher Robin, trying to keep the tail end tidy. It was the first time that the 14 turnouts had been driven together and their performance was highly commended.

Above: another view of the musical drive led by Leslie Blaze accompanied by Avril Lewis and followed by Pam Le Mottee

Above: Leslie Blaze driving Taffy with Sybella McCann in the covered wagon at the Royal Windsor Horse Show in May 1987. Milly Millington (second left) is adjusting the reigns. There was a basket of live hens in the wagon.

Above: taking part in the fancy dress at Windsor in 1984 are Paul De Vere as Prince Albert, Mary Crittall as Queen Victoria and Felicity Andrews as the footman. The Pony is Star.

Left: Some of the group's ponies stabled at the Royal Mews prior to taking part in the 1984 Lord Mayor's Show in London.

Left: Ron Hancock cadges a lift with Sarah Garnett and John Parker on the way to the start of the Lord Mayor's Show. Below: David Brand walking beside Paul De Vere driving Jack Burrill's Justin in the procession.

Above: Gill Jones driving Star with Felicity Andrews.
Below: a view from above of the RDA drivers in the Lord Mayor's show, with Ron Hancock walking beside the leading vehicle. The groom at the pony's head is Christine Cook.

Left: Yvonne Fisk with her arms round Leslie, Sean and Mark, three of the group's younger riders, at the Summer Camp in 1990.

Above: The popular pony Miss Muffett's 21st birthday celebration with her owner, Valantine Cadell.

Right: a happy young rider with his pony.

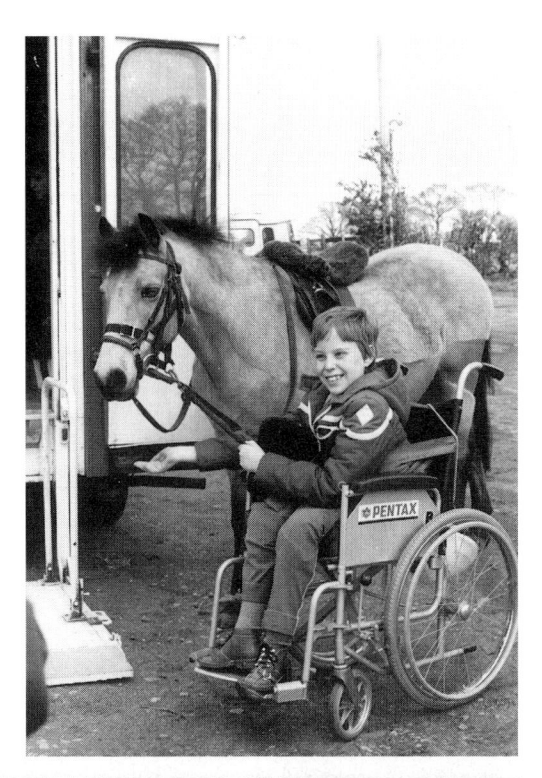

Above: Milly Millington driving her pony Little John, accompanied by Sheila Crust going through the water at hazard number 5 during the Windsor Park Sponsored Drive in 1990. There were six hazards in the 15 kilometre course which Milly did to raise money for charity.

Above: Christine David driving Little John with Sybella McCann during one of the competitions for disabled drivers.

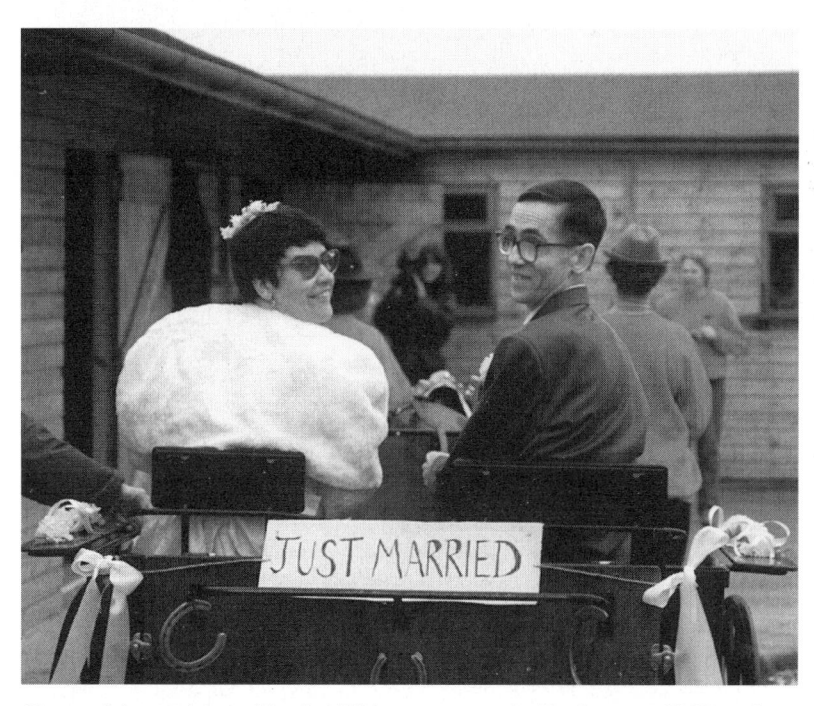

Above: John and June Morris-Wilkins were married in January 1992 and put on their wedding outfits for a special wedding party at Easter with all the drivers in the group.

Above: HRH Princess Anne presents the winning rosette to Lindsey Tyas driving Red Rascal, accompanied by Pauline Hancock with the rosettes.

Above: Neil Portsmouth driving Little John with Felicity Andrews at the RDA Show at Smith's Lawn, Windsor, in 1992.

Above: riders enjoying one of the competitions at the 1992 Summer Camp.

Above: The winning team in the inter-regional one-day event at Hartpury Agricultural College in July 1993. All four members of the South East Region team came from West Horsley. Left to right: Paul De Vere (in wheelchair), Brenda May, Judi Ralls, Shandy (the pony), Lindsey Tyas, Christine David, Paul Tyas, Red Rascal (the pony), Elizabeth Tyas.

Above: Prue Goodchild (in hat) judging one of the classes with Yvonne Fisk at the RDA Summer Camp in 1992.

Above: Richard Manning receiving his award at Arundel from Lavinia, Duchess of Norfolk. He was placed first and qualified to take part in the RDA National Championships.

Left: the blind rider Tina Smalley riding Aaron during the Christmas Ride at Wyvenhoe with Shirley (left), Amanda Beetham and Avril Ashworth.

Left: three riders from Lockwood in 1993. Jo on Blackie with Anne leading, followed by David on Magic with Philippa leading, and Tom on Marmaduke with Carol leading, going out for a ride.

Left: Dean from the Park School riding Rosie with Anne leading during a lesson in the indoor school at Wyvenhoe.

Right: Claire Cox putting a headcollar on Sparkie after returning from a ride at Wyvenhoe.

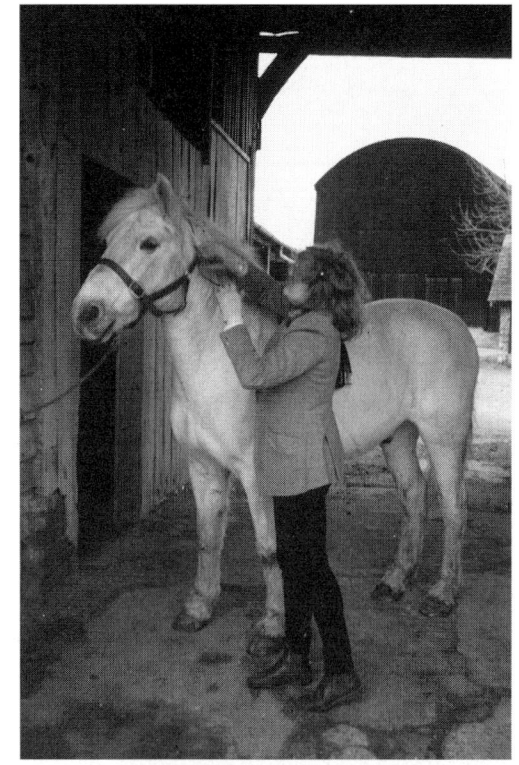

Below: HRH Princess Anne talking to Ron and Pauline Hancock before unveiling a plaque at the new tackroom at Hillside Manor Farm in 1994. In the background are Mr and Mrs Stephen Lakin, the generous owners of Hillside Manor Farm.

Above: John Vandeleur-Boorer, the retiring Chairman of the Horsley Group pats Philippa Verey's horse in the forecourt of Polsden Lacey, after she had given a remarkable demonstration of horsemanship from tacking up to advanced dressage, at the Jubilee Event in 1994.

Above: some of the large crowd of members and friends at the open day at Wyvenhoe in July 1982, who celebrated the opening of the new tack room.

Right: Judi Ralls driving her pony Shandy with Brenda May at Hartpury during the Carriage Driving Championships held in conjunction with the World Dressage Championships for handicapped riders in July 1994.

Above: the successful West Horsley team members celebrating at Hillside Manor Farm after the World Championships with their cup and rosettes. Left to right: Christine David, Lindsey Tyas, Judi Ralls and Paul De Vere.

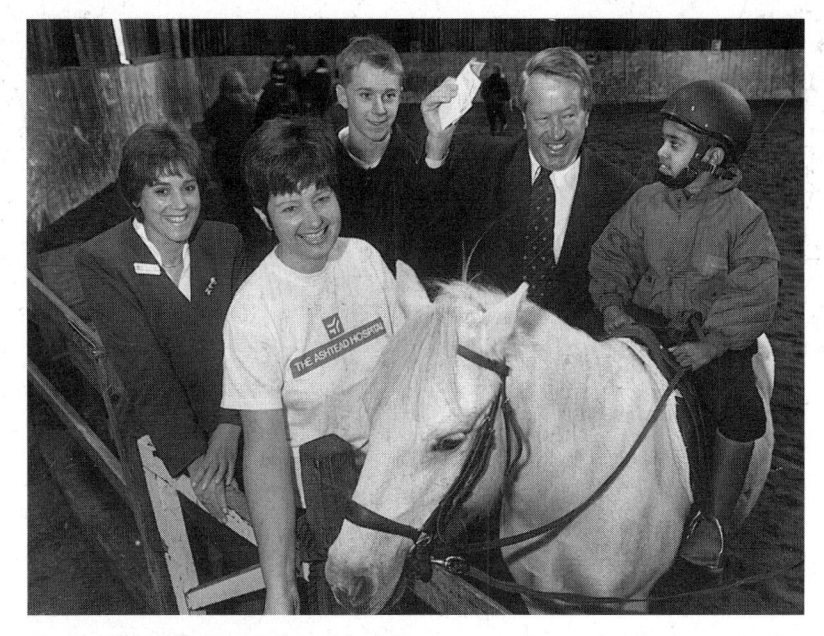

Above: Ashtead Hospital staff handing over a cheque for the group to the Chairman, Colin Wenborn, with one of the young riders, Iblal Hussan on one of the Wyvenhoe ponies.

Above: a young rider shares a carrot with her pony after a competition. The successful partnership between a pony and its rider often starts at a very young age.

96

Chapter Twelve
Medical Opinion

Among those invited to the inaugural meeting of the West Horsley Group of the RDA in November 1969 were representatives from the medical profession. Because the idea of riding with disabled people was still relatively unexplored it was considered very important that nothing was done which could be harmful in any way. It was vital that the handicapped were given the right sort of help and not pushed too far.

Conscious of the need to understand the problems of the handicapped, the group sought the advice of local physiotherapists who then made regular reports on the children's progress. The following notes were taken from a report in 1973: 'Tuesdays – These children fell mainly into two groups of paralysis – spastic and flaccid. When the children first came to us they were extremely withdrawn. In this aspect alone the improvement is marked in that there is a great deal of laughter and chatter and an air of competition is noticeable. We did not hope for miracle cures but there has been a definite strengthening of back and neck muscles, improvement of balance and during lessons muscles in spasm relax considerably. Paul, who is autistic, seemed to live for Tuesdays and we were far more 'in contact' with him by the time he left us.

'Thursdays – These children fall mainly into two groups – spina bifida and mongol (Downs Syndrome). The benefits achieved by the disabled children during riding can be enormous, not only physically but mentally as well. Fiona, aged nine, has spina bifida. When she first came to us she found sitting on a pony very difficult but the riding certainly helped strengthen her back muscles and improved her balance so that now she is able to enjoy a 10 to 15 minute ride on her pony with very little help. Matthew, aged six, is mongol. He could neither stand nor walk unaided when he first came riding and was very reluctant to leave his mother. Now he can do both these things and is quite happy going off for a ride with the helpers, leaving mother behind. The riding obviously cannot claim complete responsibility for his improvement but we all feel that it helped and hastened his ability to do these things.'

Qualified physiotherapist Patricia Rutter was one of those called on by Stella Hancock to provide advice and help during the formative years and she spent ten years as a helper. "In the beginning it was felt that a physiotherapist should be in attendance," she explains. "The group was dealing with disabled children and didn't know what was wrong with them, so it was helpful to have someone like me around who could advise them on how to hold the children, what they could and couldn't do. Nowadays riding is an accepted activity for the handicapped and it is not so important to have medical supervision.

"I always thought riding for the disabled was a brilliant idea. Most of the children who came to ride spent 80% of their time in hospital or physiotherapy departments and riding was a 'normal' activity that they could take part in, which was going to benefit them and was fun. The children had to be able to sit and support themselves, otherwise there was really no point in them riding, and we obviously had to be careful if they had hips which could dislocate easily, or similar problems.

"I made the role of physiotherapist in the group very 'low key'. I felt that it would be wrong to turn up in a white coat – the children were having a riding lesson and it had to be fun. Their medical problems must be secondary to the activity and for that reason I joined in as a helper and the children never knew I was a physiotherapist.

"We had a tremendous cross section of problems including cerebral palsy, spina bifida, Downs Syndrome and various other mental handicaps. From a physical aspect riding is very good for muscles – although with the riding periods restricted to half an hour a week its value as a strengthening exercise is limited – posture, balance and coordination. Any form of exercise is also good for the circulation, which in turn stimulates the brain.

"Although half an hour is shorter than the average riding lesson it is long enough for the majority of disabled riders for whom an hour would be too demanding both physically and mentally. A number of children were quite weak physically when they started riding and did become much stronger. They were also having treatment at physiotherapy departments so one can't say that riding was the only reason for their progress, but it certainly helped. The most important thing was that the children loved riding. Psychologically it was so good for them because it made them feel just like other children. A child with spina bifida sits in a wheelchair most of the time and to sit on a living creature which they can control with their hands is a marvellous boost.

"I felt it was important for the helpers to know what was wrong with the children. We used to hold sessions where I would describe all the different conditions that we had to deal with and tell the helpers how they could help the children and, more importantly, encourage the children to help themselves. It is important that the children have confidence in the helpers; there is a danger that they can become too dependant on one person, but once they are on a horse they must have trust in the person leading them or walking alongside.

"The greatest spin-off from riding for the disabled is the feeling of confidence that it promotes and it must never be made too difficult. It anyone takes part in an activity that they can't do then it does more harm than good. Instead of providing them with a sport that they can enjoy you are frustrating them and putting more emphasis on their disability. It must be fun."

Chapter Thirteen
Fund Raising

The initial doubts raised over the West Horsely's long term future centred on its ability to provide riding for the disabled on a regular basis. Consequently it was vital that the financial basis was sound. As Ron Hancock recalls, "We were determined that no disabled person who would benefit from riding should go short, and it was up to us to make sure this never happened."

Helpers, committee members, and for many years the instructors, gave their time for nothing but there were other expenses incurred and the responsibility for meeting these lay with the group. Any charity relies on fund raising and donations. In 1969 the West Horsley formed its first committee and with donations of £50 from the Bill Butlin Charity Trust and the Surrey County Playing Fields Association, was off and running.

In the past 25 years the group has been the recipient of gifts from various societies, clubs and organisations who have recognised the value of riding and driving to disabled people. With so many charitable causes competition for patrons is fierce and it is a tribute to the fine reputation of the West Horsley RDA group that support for their work has been continual.

The RDA has received considerable publicity through its Royal patronage and the sustained interest and support shown by The Princess Royal and the Duchess of Norfolk has done a great deal to bring the work of the association to the public's notice. A race day at Ascot raised £30,000 for the RDA and Stella Hancock was invited by Princess Anne to watch the first race from the Royal Box.

In 1975 the BBC children's television programme Blue Peter launched an appeal to raise money for the RDA with a clothes horse race. Viewers of the programme were urged to collect wool and cotton and send the material to the growing mountain in the appeal's warehouse. The West Horsley threw themselves into the cause and a horsebox full of old clothes was sent from Bookham to London. Each RDA group was invited to apply for equipment to be purchased with the money raised; some received field shelters, some saddles or other items of special equipment. The South Shields Group was given £20,000 towards the cost of an indoor school which was a fitting reward for a group that had been operating for 29 years, providing 200 rides each week with only an open field at its disposal.

The most well publicised result of the Blue Peter clothes horse appeal was the purchase of Rags, the Blue Peter pony, who was trained by three day event rider and Fellow of the British Horse Society, Tessa Martin-Bird. A grey Connemara, Rags worked with the RDA Trust at Chigwell in Essex for many years before moving to the Bridgend RDA Group. Her appearance at many fund raising events around the country provided continual publicity for the RDA and she was sadly missed after her death in 1987.

The publicity arising from the Blue Peter appeal was in some ways a mixed blessing. It raised the profile of the RDA and helped to promote its aims and achievements, but the success of the fund-raising idea led some people to believe that the association had plenty of money and wasn't in need any more. Many people are unaware, however, that the individual groups are self-financing and are responsible for their own fund-raising.

From the money raised by Blue Peter the West Horsley received a loudhailer, sheepskin saddle covers and an Australian saddle but, while all gifts were gratefully received, their most vital expenses were the day-to-day running costs of the group. Most of the equipment they needed was borrowed from Wyvenhoe. The West Horsley needed cash.

Stella Hancock was a tireless organiser of coffee mornings, sherry evenings, bring and buy sales and other fund-raising events. Hillside was the perfect location for these gatherings, providing the sort of enjoyable atmosphere that attracted people. There were always plenty of willing helpers among the wives of the farm workers and even committee meetings turned into pleasant social occasions. The need to promote the work of the group and inspire interest and support for its aims was also recognised. It was not enough to ask for money – the worthiness of the cause had to be established. With this in mind Stella Hancock, often accompanied by Sybil Atherton, gave talks at meetings of the local women's institute, inner wheel, rotary club, round table and other organisations. Videos of disabled riders were shown, articles were sent to local newspapers and support for the group soon spread throughout the area.

Two of the most effective fund raising events organised by the group were the horse show which, thanks to the generosity of Margaret and the late Jerry Howe, is still held every year at the Bookham Riding Centre, and the annual Christmas Fayre which for some time provided a major source of income. Stalls included food, bring and buy, toys, clothes, material, books, RDA items, arts, crafts and a raffle. For many years one of the most popular attractions was the large Christmas cake which Paula Stebbings would bake and then offer as a prize to anyone who could guess its correct weight.

As word of the West Horsley's work spread help was offered by other societies and individuals. The group took a stand at the Surrey County Show, the cost of which was refunded by the president of the Surrey County Agricultural Society, Raymond Stovold. In addition to the chance to educate the public the stand also provided the stage for different fund raising themes including a tombola. One year Sue Parker's grey pony Merrylegs was paraded at the show and given another name for the day which the children could attempt to guess at a cost of sixpence a time.

New fund raising ideas were a constant source of discussion at committee meetings. In October 1979 a Dress Show and Candlelight Supper was held in the elegant setting of Clandon Park. Local boutique Bernat Klein Design organised a fashion show with a team of London models and in order to reduce the costs catering for the buffet supper was undertaken by the committee – quite an effort with 300 guests to feed. Sue Parker, Carol Riley, Jilly Blake, Ann Creswell and Stella were involved in the catering team and Carol recalled mixing huge amounts of coleslaw in black dustbins. Large numbers of Black Forest gateaux were purchased wholesale, courtesy of PHAB, who ran the bar, and then had to be kept cool until the evening to prevent them from melting into a soggy mess. Despite these problems the evening was a great success; Ted Leahy put on a show of riding wear which was modelled by some of the group's supporters and proceeds from the evening of more than £3,000, were shared between the West Horsley and Surrey PHAB.

In the past the group has also benefited from fund raising on a regional level. A successful sponsored showjumping event has been held several times at Goodwood. This was won in 1976 by the West Horsley rider Samantha Gill when £4,500 was raised, half of which went to the south east regional fund. In 1981 Pam Phillips and Hugh Slater carried the flag for the West Horsley, finishing second and fourth respectively and raising a total of £320 for the group.

Sponsored rides and drives have provided a regular source of income over the years; one was even held in 1985 on the new (unopened) section of the M25 between Wisley and Leatherhead, which raised money for driving for the disabled and the British Driving Society.

The driving world has always supported the disabled drivers and in 1984 during the Derby meeting at Hickstead, Freddie Moore of Enfield sold the fruit on his winning Trade vehicle in aid of driving for the disabled. The proceeds went towards the purchase of two new Jackson Darent vehicles for disabled groups and the movement received further publicity from a demonstration by Neil Portsmouth, who then joined in the private driving class.

One of the most remarkable efforts on behalf of the RDA was that of 59 year old Joe Roberts, who undertook a 1,000 mile, nine week ride around England in aid of disabled riders and drivers. Dressed in the bright red and gold uniform of an 18th century Hussar he raised additional funds by singing and telling stories in nightclubs along the way. To the great delight of the West Horsley Joe visited the group on his way from Guildford to London, to meet the children and tell them about his journey. "The children were thrilled," recalls Sue Parker. "His visit was only arranged at the last minute but we gave him a good reception. He was marvellous with the children and they all started calling him Joe at once." So impressed was Joe with the group that he requested most of the money raised to be sent to the West Horsley for the purchase of a specially designed driving vehicle.

Another two vehicles were presented to the group in 1981, one as a result of a substantial fund raising effort by the pupils of the George Abbot School in Guildford in support of the Year of the Handicapped, and another by the Rotary Club of Bookham and Horsley.

The importance of fund raising to the group's prospects of survival was highlighted by chairman Jill Berliand at the annual general meeting in 1984. With Stella Hancock's efforts directed towards the driving section, a lack of enthusiasm and commitment was threatening the riding activities of the group and Jill Berliand called for new supporters to prevent further decline. "In any other charity it is normal for the committee to run the fund raising activities for that charity and for their friends and the general public to give generously," she reported. "The RDA is very unusual in that we work, physically, for our riders and drivers, every week of the term, and then have to raise the money to finance that activity.

"We need a fund raising sub-committee and would like to start a group of 'Friends of the West Horsley Group of the RDA'. The main committee is already stretched to its limit and at the moment there is grave danger that the groups will close. I believe in RDA and so presumably do you by your presence here, so please give this fund raising idea your utmost priority. We are in too deep to go down. Wyvenhoe depends on us and above all we have a major commitment to our riders."

Jill Berliand's appeal was answered, but 10 years later the onus of fund raising continues to lie with members of the main committee, who invariably volunteer to sit on the sub-committees of fund raising events. The annual show is still one of the main sources of income, supplemented by events such as the Jazz Festival organised by the Leatherhead Round Table in 1993, concerts, sponsored keep fit sessions, as well as a number of generous donations by local companies and individuals.

The television personality David Battie took part in an event in 1994 which attracted a large audience at Horsley. The well informed opinions he gave on the variety of interesting objects which had been brought for him to see, caused considerable interest and the very useful sum raised during the evening helped offset some of the increases in the annual expenditure.

As a result of the generosity shown by Lady Heald, an annual musical soirée is now held at Chilworth. Tricia Parker organises the catering, assisted by an enthusiastic group of volunteers, and the event also makes a substantial contribution to Group funds.

With so many charities constantly campaigning for money, fund raising has inevitably become increasingly difficult, but thanks to the continued support of the local Inner Wheel, Round Table and Rotary clubs along with generous donations from companies and a local trust, the finances of the Group are thriving again.

Chapter Fourteen
Driving for the Disabled

While thousands of handicapped people enjoy the thrill of riding, thousands more are prevented from doing so by the nature of their disability. A great deal of the benefit of riding comes from the contact with an animal, which is not confined to the physical sensation of sitting on a horse or pony.

Prince Philip has for a number of years been one of Britain's leading carriage drivers and in the early 1970s he mentioned to a helper at the Sandhurst RDA Group that driving would be an ideal sport for the handicapped who were unable to ride. This was not an entirely new idea. A small ponydrawn vehicle for those confined to wheelchairs was in existence around 1870 and can be seen at the Arlington Carriage Museum in Devon. However, the idea met with an unenthusiastic response from both the RDA and the British Driving Society (BDS) who felt that driving was too dangerous for the handicapped.

Undeterred, the Sandhurst contacted Nancy Pethick, the chairman of the Donkey Breed Society, who had recently started a driving section with her donkeys. Experiments with various types of vehicle were undertaken until with the help of Barney Thornley, a retired civil engineer, the first box-type vehicle was designed with a rear loading ramp which could accommodate a wheelchair.

Realising the danger of a group with insufficient experience setting up a separate organisation, the RDA asked Nancy Pethick to set up a trial scheme and in June 1975 the association's constitution was amended to allow groups to apply for consent to include driving for their members. Animals and vehicles had to be approved and the driving section was divided into two groups – the first for teaching the physically handicapped over the age of 16 to drive a horsedrawn vehicle, and the second for taking handicapped people out in a horsedrawn vehicle driven by a competent, able bodied driver (whip). The mentally handicapped were accepted into the second group providing they were 'immobile and not noisy' and medical consent had to be given for all drivers. Safety was regarded as the most important consideration and a safety code was drawn up by the RDA.

Princess Anne had mentioned her father's idea to Ron and Stella

Hancock during her visit to open the tack room at Wyvenhoe in 1974 and, after watching a demonstration given by Nancy Pethick and the disabled driver Neil Portsmouth during an RDA Conference at Stoneleigh in 1975 Stella drew up plans to include driving in the West Horsley group. She enlisted the help of fellow driving enthusiasts Felicity Andrews and Sarah Garnett and the three spent a day with Nancy Pethick and the Sandhurst group to learn more about the needs of disabled drivers.

The early stages of driving in the RDA were confined to donkeys, but Stella Hancock was convinced that the way ahead lay with ponies. The vehicles were little more than 'tea chests on wheels', with no room for an able bodied whip to sit alongside the wheelchair bound driver, and the animal pulling the vehicle had to be led which meant that there was little challenge for the driver.

In March 1976 Nancy Pethick came to Hillside to see the three ponies and two vehicles which Stella proposed to use. These were approved and the following year, after the inaugural meeting of the West Horsley RDA Driving Section, a committee was formed with Felicity Andrews as chairman and Stella Hancock as secretary. A purpose made vehicle designed to take a wheelchair was purchased from George Pycroft and two months later the first driving session was held at Hillside.

With space limited it was intended that priority should be given to those unable to ride but some adult members of the riding group were invited to the first session to try their hands at driving and give the committee the benefit of their thoughts and advice. Wednesday afternoons became the regular date for the driving section which started with four drivers – Pam Phillips, Yvonne Foster, Sheila Ingram and Mrs J. Slyfield. Driving began on the forestry roads of Netley Heath which were quiet and more suitable for the disabled drivers than the bumpy fields as there were no springs in the early vehicles.

To begin with the group used two ponies – one with the vehicle built to accommodate a wheelchair and the other with an exercise cart which took people who were able to be transferred from their wheelchairs. By the end of the first term the group had five drivers, who were joined by another in September. A number of others were prevented from joining in the Wednesday afternoon sessions because they worked during the day.

The West Horsley drivers were not content to walk along sedately looking at the countryside; they wanted to *drive*. For the helpers this meant running alongside as the ponies trotted along, which was exhausting for them and limiting for the drivers. A solution was provided, however, by the design of a new vehicle which could accommodate a wheelchair and an able bodied passenger who could sit alongside the disabled driver and, with the aid of a second set of reins, take control if necessary. The first vehicles were bought with money raised by a BDS drive to celebrate the Queen's Silver Jubilee in 1977, and consequently given the name Jubilee carts.

BDS members drove in relays from the south of England and Northern Ireland to Balmoral in Scotland, where they were received by The Queen and Prince Philip. The drive began in April and finished in October and involved West Horsley committee members Mary Matthews, Audrey Robinson, Felicity Andrews and Stella Hancock, as well as Alf King, who all took their turns at carrying the pennant when the relay reached the Guildford area.

The RDA committee still had to be persuaded, however. The safety code stated that disabled drivers must always be led and there were a number on the committee who felt that this rule should remain, in spite of the new vehicles. Nancy Pethick received a letter from Miss G M Walker, a physiotherapist at an Alton hospital, asking for the rule to be amended to allow vehicles accommodating an able bodied whip as passenger to be driven without a leader, because being led made the disabled driver feel restricted and inhibited. She was not keen to sanction this progressive step and appeared to see little future for the disabled driving movement. "I do not think the driving will ever be a very big undertaking," she said, "or that very many groups will be formed. It appeals to a very limited number of the disabled and is largely governed by the very limited number of competent whips needed to run the groups." Nevertheless the amendment was finally approved and the following year the West Horsley was presented with its own Jubilee cart – a vehicle designed by John Wilks and bought by Jack Burrill, the BDS Area Commissioner for Surrey who was one of the group's most enthusiastic supporters.

Off the leading rein the disabled driver was at last able to take control and really drive. The new vehicle provided a sense of freedom and gave the handicapped drivers the chance to show what they could really do. "So much more can be achieved now that the necessity of a leader can be done away with," commented Stella Hancock. The scope it created in turn led to the need for an animal with the strength and stamina to cope with longer drives. As the first group to use ponies rather than donkeys the West Horsley became a showpiece and gave numerous demonstrations to show what their drivers could achieve. With the safety aspect established more groups followed the West Horsley's lead and ponies soon outnumbered donkeys in disabled driving groups.

Thanks to the Jubilee cart driving in the West Horsley group blossomed. With Stella Hancock at the helm every opportunity to broaden the group's horizons was taken and they were invited to send two turnouts and drivers for a demonstration at the 1978 National RDA Conference. The group welcomed new drivers from the Cheshire Home at Hydon Hill, near Godalming, and by February 1979 there were 12 regular drivers taking part in the weekly sessions, which continued during the winter in the indoor school of the South Weylands Equestrian Centre. The desire of the drivers to try dressage and obstacle driving led to the need for a more comfortable vehicle to cope with the bumps of a grass arena, and springs were fitted to the Jubilee cart for which the spina bifida sufferers were particularly grateful.

In 1980 Stella Hancock and Neil Portsmouth appeared on Blue Peter to explain the benefits of driving for the handicapped. The Blue Peter pony Rags proved to be too big and strong for disabled drivers but it was considered a good idea to train her for conventional driving. The programme explained the reasons for her unsuitability for disabled driving and followed the stages of her training with Christine Dick.

As the disabled driving movement gathered momentum Stella Hancock and the West Horsley were among the figureheads and in 1980 the group broke new ground once more by organising the first ever one day event for disabled drivers, which included a one mile cross country course with five hazards. By the end of the year, which sadly saw the death of Nancy Pethick, there were 20 RDA groups with driving sections, the most active near Guildford, Ascot, Penrith and in north west Kent.

In March 1982 the separate sections of driving in the RDA were abolished and the minimum age limit of drivers was lowered to 14. It was felt that children at special schools could benefit from two years experience with an RDA group before leaving school at 16, after which they could join a BDS group if they were unable to continue with an RDA group. As teenagers young people tend to become aware of their disabilities and the limitations these can bring and driving was something they could do in spite of a disability, providing they had the use of hands, arms or voice.

Driving did, however, have the disadvantage of being an expensive sport, with vehicles costing upwards of £1,000 each and a set of harness between £500 and £600. This, together with the need for experienced able bodied whips as helpers, lack of reliable ponies and suitable venues limited the number of drivers that the group could accommodate in relation to the running costs, which caused a certain amount of friction between the driving section and the riding element. Ron Hancock made the following observation during a committee meeting in 1981: "Some may think driving is capital intensive and only a small number of drivers are involved. It *is* capital intensive but the difference it makes to those older lives, the smiles it brings to their faces, their feelings of accomplishment, has to be seen to be believed."

Finally, in 1983 it was felt that the driving section should look after its own financial affairs. With different requirements for driving and riding there had often been a conflict of interest in fund raising and the need to keep the finances separate had become apparent. "Fund raising became easier once we started to organise our own," admits Felicity Andrews. "We found fund raising easier than the riding groups as we could tell people that we wanted money for a new vehicle and then show them what their donation had helped to buy. Riding groups generally need cash for their day to day running costs but we didn't have those sort of expenses as we didn't have to pay instructors or riding schools and so on."

The Jubilee cart transformed the face of driving for the wheelchair bound but was basic in design, with a low centre of gravity, and lacked the traditional style of other conventional carriages. A new, stronger and more comfortable vehicle was needed if the disabled were to compete on equal terms with the able bodied and in 1984 Stella Hancock, who had taken over as chairman of the RDA National Driving Committee, persuaded the Worshipful Company of Coachmakers and Coach Harnessmakers to sponsor a competition at the Royal Mews to design a new vehicle for the disabled driver.

At her suggestion Neil Portsmouth was asked to join the committee of judges and he was then made chairman. The winning vehicle was the Jackson Darent, designed by Ken Jackson whose interest, enthusiasm and willingness to accept suggestions for improvement from handicapped and able bodied drivers and helpers led to further modifications and signalled the dawn of a new era for handicapped drivers.

Other carriage designers and builders also turned their attention to vehicles suitable for the disabled, leading to a number of different models, including the Horley gig for the ambulant disabled (those who could walk), specially designed for easy access and comfort; the John Willie Four Wheeler and the Bennington Super Star Buggy which had the capacity to carry a third person.

Eight years later another competition was held to design a carriage for the handicapped driver, in which the winning two wheel vehicle was awarded the RDA Stella Hancock Trophy in recognition of the founder of the original competition. The overall winner, The Getaway, designed by Devon builder Steve Phipps, reflected the need for a larger vehicle to accommodate heavier drivers. One of six four wheeled carriages to be awarded an RDA certificate, it features independently mounted, self steering front wheels, which mean that the horse remains in the same position relative to the driver, even when negotiating tight turns. Not only does this remove the risk of the vehicle jack knifing but also minimises the need for rein adjustment, something many disabled drivers with limited manual dexterity find difficult.

A report by the Stella Hancock Driving Group after one year's use stated: 'All ambulant, wheelchair and able bodied whips agree that the vehicle is very comfortable (so vital for those in wheelchairs), very stable and drives well and smoothly. It turns corners well in dressage and because the ride is so comfortable the driver can concentrate on the test. In the cones course, steering and aligning for quite a tight course was found to be no problem.'

With Stella Hancock to encourage them the West Horsley drivers went from strength to strength and by 1984 the group was operating three times a week, on Monday afternoon, Wednesday morning and Thursday evening. Shows, sponsored drives and musical demonstrations gave them the chance to show what they could achieve and they performed at events varying from the Lord Mayor's Show to Olympia and the World Carriage Driving Championships at Ascot. The BDS were persuaded to put on a class for disabled whips at their annual show at Smiths Lawn and in 1985 the first RDA Driving Show was held in the Silver Ring at Ascot. Six West Horsley drivers took part, including Millie Millington who took the show championship.

By July 1985 the number of driving groups had reached 65, a total which had grown to 87 two years later. Training days were an important part of the growth and there were six scholarships available – two given by the Nancy Pethick Memorial Fund, two by the BDS in memory of Sanders Watney, the founder and former president of the BDS, and two funded by Tony Harvey from money raised during a sponsored drive in a gipsy wagon from Suffolk to Appleby Fair in Cumbria.

The BDS scholarships were administered by the society's driving for the disabled committee which was established in 1985. Its aims were to allocate vehicles and harness to RDA groups, to find experienced able bodied whips from BDS membership to help in RDA groups and to arrange training sessions and driving holidays.

A major training breakthrough was the first two day conference and workshop held at Stoneleigh in December 1985 for members of RDA Driving Groups. Sponsored by the Medical Insurance Agency Charity and the BDS Silver Jubilee Fund (later renamed the Sanders Watney Trust) it attracted 130 delegates, 15 lecturers, and instructors and helpers from groups all over Britain who met to formulate methods and agree standards. The Medical Insurance Agency Charity later gave £20,000 to the Stella Hancock RDA Memorial Fund which now provides a considerable number of training scholarships to RDA drivers and helpers.

Stella Hancock's death in 1988 left a void in the West Horsley driving group which has never really been filled. The change of name to the Stella Hancock driving group was a fitting tribute. "In all fairness it was her group," explains Felicity Andrews. "The RDA was very frightened of driving to begin with and I don't think it would ever have got off the ground if it hadn't been for Stella. It would certainly never have got past the donkeys and walking stage."

Stella Hancock fought hard for her 'Ben Hurs' to be accepted and given the same chance as able bodied drivers. Sadly this is still being challenged with rules and restrictions imposed by over zealous, safety conscious committees. Driving trials such as the one first organised by the West Horsley in 1980 are growing in popularity amongst the disabled, but are still considered too risky in certain quarters. Felicity Andrews and Ron Hancock are two able bodied drivers who feel that the disabled deserve the chance to take part. "If they are prepared to take the risk and the people who look after them are prepared to let them, then why not?" argues Felicity Andrews. "Safety is becoming such a major concern now, but as long as every sensible precaution is taken, then why shouldn't they take part? The disabled are allowed to drive cars on public roads and are just as likely to be crashed into as anyone. Driving trials are a risk but who knows what a buzz they'll get out of it. Feeling equal is the most important thing."

The battle for quality that has been fought on behalf of the disabled by people like Stella Hancock was challenged again by a directive which made it compulsory for disabled drivers to wear crash helmets at all times. This is a sensible precaution for the marathon phase of a driving trial but would certainly have detracted from the elegance of turnouts in showing classes and dressage events. As a result this has now been amended and dressage competitions, concours d'élégance and show classes are now excluded from this restriction, for the disabled just as for able bodied competitors.

A move to separate the driving from the main body of the RDA has its supporters, who feel that driving for the disabled would benefit from a committee of driving people who would be safety conscious but perhaps not so blinkered in their vision. There are currently only two driving representatives on the RDA committee and there are many in the driving movement who feel that this is insufficient representation.

However, the fight for equality continues. The Stella Hancock group, while continuing to miss the energy and innovation of its principal founder, is flourishing and recording further successes in competitions around the country. Now run by Brenda May as secretary following the retirement of Felicity Andrews in 1992, it has a permanent base at Hillside thanks to the generosity of the new owner Stephen Lakin, who not only allows them access to his land but also laid down an area of concrete on which the group has constructed a portable building, which gives them a dry and warm meeting place for the winter and a store for their vehicles.

Sessions are held on Wednesday and Friday mornings, after which drivers and helpers often retire to the local pub. The spirit of Stella Hancock lives on, typified by the words of Felicity Andrews, reflecting on her 15 year involvement with the group, "We all just had a bloody good time."

Chapter Fifteen
The 'Ben Hurs'

The members of the Stella Hancock group vary considerably in age and handicaps but all derive a considerable amount of pleasure and achievement from being 'in control'. Paul de Vere has been with the group since it began; physically handicapped from birth, he is confined to a wheelchair and doesn't have full use of his hands, but driving gives him the sense of freedom that the able bodied take for granted. When he has the reins not only is he responsible for his own safety but also that of his passenger, and for that time at least he is in control of his own destiny.

The term 'disabled' implies someone who lacks the ability to use the full range of their physical and mental faculties. The Oxford dictionary qualifies a disability as 'a thing that disables or disqualifies a person'. There is a saying that 'everyone has some ability but some are more able than others' and in the same way it could be said that everyone has some disability but some are more disabled than others.

The discrimination against disabled people manifested itself in 1977 when the West Horsley was asked to provide a pony to receive a vehicle and harness at the Olympia Christmas Show on behalf of the RDA. Despite the support of show director Raymond Brooks-Ward, the group was refused permission by the BDS for one of its disabled drivers to take part in the presentation. In a letter to Raymond Brooks-Ward, Stella Hancock referred to the visit by Princess Anne in 1974, when all the members of the West Horsley riding group came into the school at Wyvenhoe mounted. "This was a mistake," wrote Stella, "as the majority of our visitors did not realise how handicapped the children were until one boy had to be lifted off his pony and put into his wheelchair. By the same token, if we have able bodied drivers at Olympia we feel that the point will be lost."

Stella Hancock fought hard to bring general acceptance for her disabled friends and gave many talks and demonstrations to illustrate that a handicap should never be used to judge a person. Everyone is disabled in some way, whether by an eye problem which requires spectacles, defective hearing, lack of hand and eye coordination or simply an inability to master a particular skill.

"We must beware of the danger of having a preconceived picture in our minds of the 'disabled driver'," she said. "For there is as big a range of difference amongst those who are classified as disabled as amongst those who are not. Both classes – if you allow the distinction – contain skilful and unskilful people. Not all disabilities can be overcome. What is needed is a sensible appraisal of the degree of disability and an acceptance of the limitations it imposes, while using every sensible means of overcoming them."

This ability to overcome handicaps was illustrated in 1983 when a group of thalidomide children visited the West Horsley group to have a go at driving. Most drove with their feet, using the special reins with loops designed for those with limited manual dexterity, but Stella Hancock reported afterwards that some of the achievements made during the day were quite outstanding.

Many of the requisites for carriage driving are similar to those of driving a car, most notably the ability to concentrate and anticipate trouble. "Driving is more dangerous than riding," explained Stella Hancock. "Unless you are constantly alert you do not get the warnings that come sooner to those sitting on the horse's back. The ability to concentrate is important and the failure to do so ranks as a disability. The able bodied whip has to be as fully aware of his companion's powers of concentration as he has to be aware of any physical disability."

Disabled driving groups do not exclude the mentally handicapped but it is important that they do not detract from the enjoyment and progress of the physically handicapped. The joy of driving is that, with the use of hands and voice, an otherwise physically handicapped person can achieve a high level of skill which matches that of an able bodied whip. For this reason the experienced physically handicapped drivers do not want to drive with the mentally handicapped.

"The driving group is very social," agrees Felicity Andrews. "Everyone is equal and the fact that some are in a wheelchair is totally forgotten. They are just a group of people doing what they enjoy. Several physically handicapped drivers said, 'We are not mentally handicapped and we don't want to be grouped with them.' Rightly or wrongly I don't see what the very mentally handicapped would gain from driving. Although the movement of the vehicle and the contact with other people is beneficial you don't have the same physical contact with the pony as you do when riding. A driver is more aloof from the pony and you don't get the warmth and stimulation of sitting on its back."

In the early days of disabled driving the BDS Council was unanimous in its decision to recommend that driving was confined to the physically handicapped, and an application by the West Horsley to include section II of the RDA Driving in its constitution and so accept mentally handicapped members encountered fierce opposition from Nancy Pethick, who was the BDS representative on the RDA Council, and fellow BDS

Council member Anne Norris. "I feel it is essential to have mentally bright people who will do as they are told without question and as soon as they are requested," explained Anne Norris, while Nancy Pethick argued, "I feel it is not of much use as a therapy for the (mentally) disabled and the risks far outweigh any advantages."

The invitation to Stella Hancock to join the BDS sub-committee on safety was subsequently withdrawn but the West Horsley won their battle and no longer had to discriminate against those with a mental handicap, however slight. Despite their early disagreements regarding driving and the mentally handicapped – some of which were strongly held – Nancy Pethick, Anne Norris and Stella Hancock became good friends and Anne Norris in particular became a close ally of the West Horsley founder.

While unwilling to prevent the mentally handicapped from driving, even Stella Hancock had her doubts concerning the benefits gained. After visiting one group of drivers she commented: "Of the six who arrived the day I was there only two could communicate with a form of speech and I began to wonder who was going to benefit from this whole performance. I believe our job is to teach people to drive and that we are not there for costly 'people sitting'. However, by the end of the day this doubting Thomas saw the flicker of light. The youngsters did communicate their pleasure, which the group members were good at translating, and the super care staff were thrilled to see their charges stimulated by this new activity."

Spastics are often seen as mentally handicapped, due to their speech difficulties and awkward convulsive movements, but it is a physical disability. Felicity Andrews recalls one young girl who was sent to the group from the White Lodge Spastic Centre. "She was absolutely terrified when she first came and only wanted to watch. One day I persuaded her to let us wheel her into the vehicle and then take her straight out again. The following week she stayed in the vehicle for a little longer and very gradually she started to do a bit more each week. For a long time we were driving the pony for her but after two or three years she became very competent, learnt to drive a cones course and began to sit much more upright. She adored her driving and although she found speaking difficult she learnt to communicate with the ponies and tell them to walk or trot on."

In 1984 the RAF rehabilitation centre at Chessington and later Headley Court near Leatherhead began to send patients to drive with the group. All had been disabled as a result of accidents, some during the Falklands War or in action elsewhere with the forces, but a large number in road accidents. Those handicapped as a result of injury are often more difficult to deal with than those disabled from birth and Ron Hancock recalls that many of the patients were not immediately willing to try a new activity. "Some of them merely lay on the ground shouting and the physiotherapists who had come with them told us to ignore them. Most were young people in their 20s or 30s who had either had their legs blown off by mines or been injured in motor bike accidents. Those that were 'bolshie' were usually encouraged by the others into having a go and suddenly they would be driving across a field, looking over hedges and realising that they could still do things that they had been able to do before their accidents. The physiotherapists all remarked that they were then much easier to handle and adopted a different attitude to life."

"We did have some remarkable successes with the patients from Headley Court," Felicity Andrews recalls. "One particular chap had been left physically and mentally scarred and had not spoken since his accident. The physiotherapists had tried everything to make him talk and then one day we said to him, 'If you want this pony to move you've got to say walk on, otherwise he's going to stand here all day'. After a minute or two we heard a grunt and then a sound like 'walk on' and I quietly flicked the whip so the pony walked on. The man was so chuffed and gradually began to talk again.

"We also had a wonderful Gurkha who drove with us for a time. He had been injured in a road accident in Hong Kong but the army paid for his rehabilitation at Chessington. He adored driving and became very good. We've always been very keen that our members really do drive properly and we teach them to do the best they can."

The sense of achievement associated with learning to drive a pony has transformed many lives. Jane was born with a severely deformed spine and had spent the 21 years of her life in a wheelchair. During a driving session she took her very nervous mother for a drive around the indoor school and was thrilled as it was the first time she had been able to do something that her mother couldn't. Susan had severe congenital deformities of her legs and had spent her life in institutions, often having to spend the day in bed due to staff shortages. Driving added a new dimension to her life and her greatest moment came when she took part in a driving demonstration. The organisers offered sherry to all those taking part and as a result a very giggly Susan drove with even greater confidence. Twenty five year old John had a progressive muscular disorder and rarely had much to say until he started driving. The boost to his self confidence was considerable and helped him to participate in a public discussion on disabled driving.

One woman who developed a notable talent for driving was Sheila Ingram. Severely handicapped from birth and wheelchair bound, she had been unable to cope with riding but became a founder member of the driving section of the West Horsley RDA. Sheila epitomised all Stella Hancock's hopes for the disabled and her determination to succeed was a inspiration to everyone. Not content with RDA one day events and driving classes she also enjoyed the BDS rallies when she could drive on equal terms with the able bodied whips.

Winner of the BDS Trophy for disabled drivers at the annual Smiths Lawn show in 1981, she repeated that success the following year, to which she added the Bianca Sergeant Memorial Trophy for the best handicapped driver in the obstacle competition at the Brockham Harness Club's annual show and the championship for disabled drivers at the national ride and drive show. Tragically she died later that year at the age of 28.

The loss of members is something that every RDA group has to face as many handicapped people have shorter life expectancies than the able bodied, due to the nature of their illness. 'Mike' Parsons sadly died before she was able to fulfil her wish to drive at the BDS Show but her family and friends donated money to the group which went towards the purchase of a vehicle in her memory.

Another star of the group has been Millie Millington, who underwent major surgery on her spine following an accident. Having started with the riding group of the West Horsley in 1983 she was soon persuaded to join the driving section by Stella Hancock, who knew that Millie had driven trade and farm vehicles in her teens. "Life just snowballed from there," Milly recalls, "and my whole world has changed for the better. I have met some wonderful people and been privileged to drive some grand horses and ponies."

Her many competition successes include the disabled drivers championship at the 1985 BDS Show and the show championship at the first RDA Driving Show, and she has taken part in numerous demonstrations and musical drives. Sponsored by the group, Millie spent a week with Caroline Dale and returned with her BDS Grade II. Further proof of her skill has been provided by her notable successes against able bodied whips driving her ex-racing donkey stallion Dodo. She has also been a great fund raiser for the group and an enthusiastic contributor to the organisation of many of its special events.

Only the disabled can accurately gauge their own improvement and Stella Hancock consulted her own drivers before suggesting the following benefits of carriage driving to the handicapped: 'Muscle tone – the use of different muscles when driving from those used to rotate the wheelchair wheels. Posture – people in wheelchairs, especially those with spinal injuries, are not inclined to sit up. If you drive a dressage test or compete in the show ring you have to sit tall to catch the judge's eye, as if to say 'Look at me, I'm good'. Coordination – for those who can hold the reins and use them correctly it subconsciously encourages finger movement. Motivation – driving has motivated them and sharpened their reactions. Some never experienced competition as children; driving has filled this gap and they enjoy the great feeling of challenge'.

Disabled drivers in RDA groups are never allowed to drive alone or with another handicapped person and must always be accompanied by an experienced able bodied whip. Some drivers do, however, have their own turnouts and drive privately at home, like Stella Hancock member Judi Ralls who brings her pony to group sessions where other members can also have the pleasure of driving him. Judi competes successfully in private driving and one day events, the thrill of driving more than compensating for the headache which frequently results from the activity.

The aim of RDA driving groups is integration, giving its disabled drivers the chance to share their sport with able bodied whips, and the BDS welcomes the disabled at rallies and picnic drives. While the opportunity to compete has fulfilled many ambitions, just as many disabled people have simply welcomed the chance to enjoy the sights and sounds of the countryside and the feel of the wind on their faces.

Harriet Howard suffers from Achondraplasia which hinders the growth of arms and legs, and enjoys the adrenalin produced by the cross country phase of driving trials. Nevertheless she says, "A lot of the appeal of driving is the rapport one has with the pony and the friendship and loyalty it gives you back. One of the nicest things is driving alone with one's pony, just me and it chatting away to each other."

"If you do not want to compete it does not mean that you are any less of a driver," maintained Stella Hancock. "It is important that people should be taught to drive for enjoyment. This means that people who just like driving should be taught to drive safely and gain confidence. They don't have to beat anyone else. Some teachers are more competitive than their pupils and encourage expectations which often cannot be attained. You do your pupil no service if he has to suffer for the failure of your aspirations."

Perhaps the real essence of a horse and carriage is expressed in the sentiments of one 60 year old man, disabled from birth, who said, "I do so enjoy the physical delight of driving around the countryside, controlling legs that really work."

Chapter Sixteen
Donkeys and Dreams

Forty five year old Neil Portsmouth has been confined to a wheelchair since the age of two. Muscular dystrophy has severely restricted his physical mobility but has in no way diminished his spirit or his determination to live his life in the able bodied community. Limited use of his hands has not prevented him from producing some fine landscape paintings, a hobby he is now reserving for his 'old age'.

A love of animals and horses in particular resulted in attempts at riding with one of the early RDA groups but his life changed dramatically when he was introduced to driving donkeys by Nancy Pethick, which led to a meeting with Stella Hancock and the chance to benefit from her determination to let handicapped drivers compete on equal terms with able bodied whips. Driving became more than a form of recreation for Neil, it developed into a skill which has earned him the admiration and respect of top class able bodied drivers from all over the world. His many competition successes were crowned by winning the coveted disabled drivers championship at the BDS Show in 1990 and three years later he was elected to the RDA Driving Committee – one of the very few disabled people to become a member of the governing body.

In his own words Neil explains the part played in his life by driving and the benefits of the sport to the disabled.

*   *   *

"I became involved with riding for the disabled at the age of 17, before the RDA was formed. Initially I rode, which I did for about 12 years, but as it became more difficult for me to get on and off the horse the group I was with – the South Bucks – suggested that I got in touch with Nancy Pethick, who had just started using her donkeys to drive disabled people and had a cart specially designed to take a wheelchair.

"Driving answered all the problems I had of sitting on a horse. All I would ever be able to achieve as a rider was sitting on a pony's back and being led around a field, and because my balance was so bad I had to be held on. Driving was something I could do from my wheelchair which still gave me the contact with horses that I loved.

"As the riding became more difficult, so the driving progressed. I first met Stella Hancock at Stoneleigh, where Nancy and I gave a demonstration at an international RDA Conference, and following another meeting at Reading where Nancy and I gave another demonstration, Stella asked me to come and drive with the group she had just started. Driving with donkeys was accepted by then but Stella wanted to take it one step further and use ponies, which had more scope and were more fun to drive.

"Stella and I became great friends and we gave a number of demonstrations to attract publicity for driving for the disabled. Driving gave me a sense of freedom and a psychological feeling of being in control of my own destiny – as much as anyone can be with a horse or pony. The freedom was matched by the sense of achievement produced by mastering an animal. The unpredictable element gives it the 'kick' and we must be careful not to lose that. If driving for the disabled is suffering from anything at the moment it is that some people are trying to make it so safe and clinical that the fun element is going out of it. The element of risk provides the adrenalin which makes driving such fun.

"I know you need rules and regulations, particularly with the riding where you have mentally handicapped people who have no perception of danger, but if we have the intelligence and ability to drive a horse then surely we have the right to choose whether or not to take the risks involved. At the moment, the RDA seems to want to think for me. This implies that I am not capable of taking responsibility for myself and I find that insulting because for my whole life I have fought against just that, by being a disabled person in an able bodied world. Through Stella Hancock and Nancy Pethick driving became accepted as something the disabled could do on equal terms with the able bodied and now I feel they are trying to take away our freedom of thought.

"I know when something is too dangerous for me and I know my own capabilities. For instance I have never wanted to drive without an able bodied passenger with me as I know that if the pony started misbehaving badly I wouldn't be strong enough to deal with it. A disabled person with the full use of their hands and arms probably could but I can't grip the reins in the conventional way. I have loops in the reins that I put my hands through, so shortening the reins quickly is difficult. When you are in a wheelchair that is tied to the floor of the vehicle you are a million times more vulnerable anyway so it's nice to know that you've got someone there who can sort out the pony if necessary. I know I couldn't cope on my own.

"Stella was always looking for new challenges for her drivers and she used people all over the country as sounding boards to bounce ideas off. I've always lived my life in the able bodied community and so it was possibly easier for her to talk to me than to someone who has become institutionalised. The access that driving provides is invaluable. If, like me, you are disabled and haven't got the strength to push your wheelchair over uneven ground it is very difficult to go out into the countryside. When you're in a wheelchair you are never more than four feet high, even if you're a six feet tall man, so it's no good wondering what is on the other side of a hedge unless you ask someone. When you are driving you can see over the hedge and all it takes is a gentle pull on the reins to go and look at something."

"I didn't realise I was a competitive person until I started driving with Stella. I had never previously had the urge or need to do something better than anyone else and perhaps that is something I did miss by being brought up in an able bodied community. Because I grew up with able bodied friends I had the feeling that there wasn't much point trying to do things as I'd never do them as well as they did. Driving was something that I felt I could do and Stella encouraged me to try.

"I never realised I had the urge to win until I managed to drive around a course of cones faster than anyone else without knocking one down and someone gave me a rosette for doing it. You couldn't get my head into a bowler hat for a week! I would like to have a go at driving trials but dressage is my main interest. I also like showing; I know it's a bit 'poncey' but I like to dress up. I think I'm basically a show-off.

"Driving isn't easy but that is why it is a challenge. Lengthening and shortening the reins with any speed is difficult for me. To drive well you need to be able to do it in half a second and it take me three or four seconds which is why I'm always at a disadvantage driving a cones course. If I'm up against someone with the full use of their hands then the chances are they will beat me because their manual dexterity will be better than mine. My greatest sense of achievement is when I manage to beat them.

"My manual dexterity hasn't improved but driving has kept me physically more active. My back, arms and shoulders are, if not stronger, then still working, which they wouldn't be otherwise. Physiotherapy is all very well but it's not the same as taking part in a sport. Driving gives me physical exercise but also the mental agility and a psychological boost. If you're in a physiotherapy class you're doing exercises but you're always aware that the reason you're doing them is that you are disabled and you've got to do them in order to keep fit and active enough to cope with life. When I'm driving, I'm driving – just like everyone else.

"The physical benefit is almost secondary to the actual feeling of driving. That is what makes it so important – it gives me a sense of normality. I'm doing something that a lot of able bodied people can't do and even some of those that can, can't do it as well as me. It's a bit of oneupmanship.

"Driving also means being accepted in an able bodied world. Very skilled driving people appreciate what we do and that means a lot. John Parker, the brilliant coachman who does so much to help disabled drivers, once told me that I drive dressage better than he does, which is one of the greatest compliments I could ever receive. He meant it genuinely as well and I think that is the greatest thing I've found about the driving world – it is far less patronising than any other sporting activity I've been involved with.

"Many disabled people, especially ambulants, do not appear disabled when they are driving, which is why it is such a good sport for the handicapped. I can't carry a whip but I'm still using the same aids as a normal driver – my hands and voice. When you're riding if you can't use your legs and seat then you're not going to achieve very much, but when you're driving you're on the same terms as everyone else and very few sports offer that for the disabled.

"The contact with an animal is the greatest attraction to me of driving. I love horses and to have the chance to be involved with them and to train them is wonderful. When you have spent hours trying to get an extension out of a rather stiff animal and then you get three lengthened strides it is like winning a gold medal.

"Thanks to Stella Hancock I have achieved everything I ever wanted to but I would like to drive a pair. To really feel that I was giving it my best shot, however, I would need to stay in my wheelchair and a vehicle has not yet been designed for a pair that will take a wheelchair. People think it must be marvellous to be taken out of my wheelchair, but it isn't. My wheelchair is my home; I've lived in it for 43 years and I don't feel safe if I'm taken out of it to sit in a vehicle. I'm like a fish out of water.

"I would also like to be more involved with driving at a governing level. I am the only disabled person on the RDA Driving Committee. There should be a greater representation but people should be chosen on account of their experience and commitment to driving and not simply because they are disabled."

Chapter Seventeen
The Real Heroes

Driving groups affiliated to the RDA need to meet strict requirements laid down by the association, which involve experienced able bodied whips, a sufficient number of helpers, a suitable venue, approved ponies or donkeys, safe well maintained harness including looped reins, and approved vehicles. When these are assembled, the group must familiarise itself with the equipment and the procedures of harnessing up and putting to, loading and unloading wheelchairs, and the experienced whips must instruct the helpers in driving techniques and safety procedures.

The disabled driver needs the skill of an experienced and capable able bodied whip to be able to enjoy the thrill of driving, whether in a field, woods or show ring. Novice drivers are a great asset but it is only experienced whips who can drive with and teach the disabled. The horsedrawn carriage is a greater potential hazard than the ridden horse. At any time an emergency could arise which must be dealt with quickly and efficiently to avoid an accident. For this reason the able bodied whip also has a set of reins when accompanying a disabled driver. If the driver becomes tired or is in danger of losing control the able bodied whip can immediately take over with the minimum of fuss.

"Able bodied whips with RDA driving groups have to really know what they are doing and be capable drivers," explains Felicity Andrews. "When accompanying a disabled driver there is a fine line between interfering and being safe. With an experienced disabled whip I would never take over the reins unless they asked me to but with some drivers you do occasionally feel that they are not quite in control and then you must take over in the interests of safety."

Neil Portsmouth agrees that the able bodied whip must step in if necessary. "They must know when to take over. When accompanying a competent disabled driver, a good whip will not interfere unless asked, but with an inexperienced driver who possibly won't appreciate that he is in trouble until it is too late, the whip must step in before control is lost. It is necessary to have a rapport between the able bodied whip and the disabled driver and a knowledge of the driver's disability and experience. I've had a lot of experience now. I'm used to horses and I can sometimes anticipate a problem before the able bodied whip."

A number of Britain's leading carriage drivers, including former world champion George Bowman, are tremendous supporters of disabled driving and happily give their time and advice to groups. Although experienced whips are needed to drive with the disabled, willing volunteers who have no driving background are also welcome to act as grooms and hold the ponies while they are being harnessed up and put to the vehicle; manoeuvre the wheelchair bound drivers up the ramp into the vehicle, help the ambulant drivers to climb in and generally assist from the ground.

The need for training helpers has long been recognised by the RDA driving committee and training days are organised throughout the country, where harnessing up, putting to, loading wheelchairs and safety rules are demonstrated. Part of the training involves sitting in a wheelchair while it is loaded into a vehicle to provide a better understanding of the disabled drivers' needs and the problems of the wheelchair bound. In addition to the training days, a considerable number of scholarships are available every year for helpers to spend some time with an experienced driver and increase their level of skill.

Helpers are encouraged to work for and take the BDS Carriage Driving Test One which requires a knowledge of stable management equivalent to Pony Club 'C' test level and the ability to drive a single turnout. One thing helpers must do is concentrate on what they are doing. Carelessness leads to mistakes and safety is paramount when dealing with horsedrawn vehicles, whether driven by the handicapped or able bodied.

The chance to help others clearly brings its own reward but many of the helpers with the Stella Hancock Group have, through their involvement, experienced unique occasions like the Lord Mayor's Show. As Felicity Andrews acknowledges, "I have done things through driving for the disabled that I would never have done otherwise. I also get a tremendous buzz out of helping the physically handicapped drivers because I am helping people to achieve something and that is very satisfying."

Jack Burrill spoke for many helpers when, in 1981, he said, "I know we are in a depressed situation. For most of us it will get better, but not I'm afraid for the disabled and that is why I would like to do something while I still can." Despite a full time job as transport manager for Sainsburys, Jack Burrill, who died in 1992, always found time to lend a helping hand wherever it was needed.

The generosity of the willing volunteers who run the driving groups is never taken for granted by the disabled whips, but to many the real heroes are the ponies, whose endless patience and cooperation provide so much enjoyment. An RDA driving pony must be thoroughly reliable and obedient under all conditions, responsive to the aids of voice, hands and whip and have good driving manners.

Every pony and donkey used in an RDA driving group has to be inspected and approved before it can be used and the unsuitable are rejected. Sarah Garnett is one of the RDA inspectors and applies the same rigid code of obedience to RDA ponies that she insists on with her own competition winning tandem. "Ponies must be obedient," she explains. "In driving, everyone's life depends on the pony doing what it is told. Obedience to the command to stand immobile is the most important because in the event of anything happening, if the pony stands completely still, there is no problem."

In the early days of disabled driving the ideal size for an RDA pony was between 11.2 and 13.2 hh, as the vehicles used were generally about 18 inches from the ground and the drivers couldn't see over the quarters of an animal more than 14 hands high. However, the improvements in design have led to an increase in the variety of carriages available for handicapped drivers and requirements are now growing for larger animals to pull the bigger four wheeled vehicles designed for heavier drivers which are now approved by the RDA. Temperament has always been more important than size and the animal must be in regular work to prevent any misbehaviour through freshness.

Donkeys were originally considered to be safer for disabled drivers because when frightened their instinct is to 'freeze' whereas a pony in the same situation tends to bolt. Stella Hancock's view that ponies would provide the disabled with greater enjoyment and challenge was reinforced by a visit to Nancy Pethick's donkey driving group, accompanied by Sarah Garnett and Felicity Andrews. "During our visit we drove the donkeys," Felicity recalls, "and I had never before driven an animal which had its head pointing the opposite way to which it was going! You could bring its head round to the right and it would still go left."

The West Horsley driving section got underway with four privately owned ponies which were all driven regularly by their owners at home and in combined driving events, a policy that Felicity Andrews still endorses. "I'm convinced that it is best to use privately owned ponies. We did at one time have a couple of group owned ponies but someone then has to look after them and they don't get the amount of work that they need or the variety which stops them getting bored. Driving is more hazardous than riding, which is usually indoors and involves someone leading the pony. Most drivers, and certainly the ones in our group, want to really drive and compete on equal terms so the ponies have to be 200% reliable. If they are driven out and about regularly by their owners they are much better behaved during the disabled driving sessions whereas if they were bored or short of work they might decide 'whoopee I'm off' and that could be disastrous."

Although obedience is vital the ponies need to be forward going enough to give an enjoyable drive and many have endeared themselves to the drivers with their character and spirit. One of the first ponies used by the West Horsley drivers was Stella Hancock's Prince, who was later sold to the group and renamed Sainsburys Prince following the donation of £500 for his purchase by the supermarket giants. When he had to be put down in 1982 after a severe bout of laminitis the response from the public was overwhelming. Donations towards the cost of replacement came from companies, schools, scouts, old age pensioners, the Leatherhead and District Lions, Banstead Hospital Centenary Association and Sutton Adult School Bingo Club. The most remarkable fund raising effort was by 82 year old Fred Pike, who collected almost £200 as the result of a sponsored swim. Following a countrywide search a new recruit was found in Devon – a seven year old Welsh liver chestnut mare called Sunshine, whose gentle temperament soon made her a favourite with the group.

Jack Burrill's Justin was also one of the mainstays in the formative period and gave years of faithful service to the disabled whips. Paul de Vere recalls driving him around a cones course against the clock at a national show, accompanied by a lady whip while Jack Burrill watched from the crowd. "I couldn't get much speed out of Justin, no matter how many times I shouted 'trot! trot!'," laughs Paul. "Suddenly there came a screeching whistle from the crowd. Justin recognised his owner's call, pricked up his ears and took off like a rocket. Twice I nearly lost my whip on the corners but we ended up with a clear round and a cup for the fastest time."

The use of the voice as the principal aid in driving inevitably results in recognition by ponies of their owner's voice and they will usually respond more rapidly to a familiar tone. The trust that develops between pony and driver is an important safety factor and provides a valuable element of confidence. "I've never been worried driving with a disabled whip," Felicity Andrews admits, "because I've always used my ponies and had complete faith in them. I know that they will respond to me whoever is driving them. It is important for the able bodied whip to know the pony and for the pony to listen to them in case of problems."

A responsive pony increases the driver's enjoyment. Paul de Vere can bear testament to this following a national dressage and cones event at Royal Windsor. "For this event I drove a little firecracker called Little John," he recalls. "The dressage went like a dream; he was so light to drive and I could even rein back four paces without using any harsh words or needing any assistance from Helen, my able bodied whip. I was wondering how he would go in the cones but I got no further than the 't' in 'trot on' before he was off like a bullet. He seemed to know exactly where he was going and although I nearly lost Helen at the third bend we finished with a clear round. I came second in both events and received the Little John Trophy as overall champion in the non ambulant class.

The trophy was presented by Millie Millington and named after her pony Little John – 'the first and the best', she assured me. It was a double blessing to have won the cup with a pony of the same name."

The grey Welsh pony Taffy, bought from Joe Pullen in 1982, was owned by the group but driven regularly by Stella Hancock. He was a great character and another that Paul de Vere remembers with great affection. "I once drove him at a combined driving event and was approaching the final obstacle which was a water splash, when dear old Taffy decided to go backwards and tried to put us up a tree. We think that he noticed his previous owner who happened to be a judge at the obstacle. Bless him! He definitely had a mind of his own."

The willingness of horses and ponies to respond to people is more than blind obedience and the occasional shows of independence merely inspire affection in the true horse lover. The Princess Royal summed it up perfectly when she spoke of 'the love and respect horse and rider have for each other'. It is a feeling which also encompasses the driver – handicapped or able bodied.

Chapter Eighteen
A View from Both Sides

On March 13, 1980, Paul and Elizabeth Tyas experienced every parent's nightmare when their four year old daughter Lindsey was hit by a car while crossing the road and knocked unconscious. Her other injuries included a ruptured liver, broken femur, punctured lung and bruised kidneys. Even more alarmingly, however, she had lost the use of her right arm and leg.

Lindsey had been riding since the age of eleven months and it was already an important part of her life. While in intensive care she was stimulated into moving her right hand by the offer of a red rosette from her consultant, but when she left hospital after an eighteen week stay, her parents were told that she must never ride again.

In her own words, Lindsey explains how carriage driving provided her with a new challenge, and her mother Elizabeth describes her involvement with the Stella Hancock Group.

*   *   *

"I am lucky to be alive," says Lindsay Tyas. "When I was four years old I was knocked down by a car and paralysed down my right side and when the time came for me to leave hospital, the consultant told my parents that one of the things I was never to do again was ride.

"Even though I was only four my love for horses had already been formed, as I had spent most of my short life running around my mother's riding stables. I *had* to ride again.

"I was lucky that mum and dad allowed me that wish as at the age of 18 I still love horses and have also been introduced to carriage driving. In 1986 my parents bought a ride and drive pony called Red Rascal and it was through him that my enjoyment for this exciting sport developed.

"The first time I was introduced to the Stella Hancock Group was on a breezy summer day during my school holidays. The poppies were swaying in the wind in the nearby field and gathered under a big oak tree was a group of about a dozen people, some in wheelchairs. The ponies were ready and a few people were already being helped in to the vehicles whilst others waited their turn and chatted over cups of coffee.

"I was introduced to the group by my mother, who had been a helper there for several months and had asked me if I wanted to go and help with the ponies and perhaps have the chance to drive. The first pony I drove was Pauline Farino's palomino mare "Bubbly". She was lovely and I felt quite privileged to drive her as she had previously been used as part of Pauline's tandem in FEI driving trials. I never imagined then that I would actively compete in competitions with the group as one of their drivers.

"My first outing with the Stella Hancock Group was at the Ham polo ground, where they gave a musical drive display to promote driving for the disabled. I drove the group's own pony Taffy – a Welsh mountain – and my able bodied whip was a lady called Sue Henderson.

"During term time, school has prevented me from being able to drive at the group's weekly meetings, but I have been lucky enough to compete in the group competitions, even more so after Red Rascal was passed as an RDA pony. I have competed at various shows such as the Surrey Area Show at Bookham, Royal Windsor, and the RDA Show which is held annually at Smith's Lawn. I was also fortunate to be given the chance to compete as a member of the South East team at the first Inter Regional Carriage Driving event at Wimpole Hall. Each team consisted of four drivers selected from regions all over the country, competing in dressage and cones. The Stella Hancock Group had two drivers selected, and Carol Lee and I teamed up with two members of the Herons Ghyll Group, Karen Baker and Russell Barton.

"Our team completed the day very successfully, winning the championship, with Carol Lee deservedly winning the dressage. It was at this event that a vote was taken to add hazards to the competition. I have now competed in three Inter Regional events and in the last, at Hartpury, the marathon section consisted of several hazards that looked similar to those you would find in an FEI event, which made the day really exciting!

"The highlight of my driving career so far came in 1990 when I won one of the Harpers and Queen's Scholarships. I was presented with the award at the Horse of the Year Show, where I was lucky enough to drive John Parker's Andalusian stallion Piconero. I went on to spend my scholarship at John Parker's yard, where I drove various combinations of his Hungarian horses and Susan Townsend's Connemarras. All these experiences have led me to produce a promotional video for the Stella Hancock Group as part of my A level communications course work. I am hoping to go on to do a horse studies course at Bicton College, which will hopefully lead to a horse-related career.

"Driving has enabled me to achieve many goals – notably to compete in one day events and drive at Wembley. I hope one day to be able to represent Britain in a driving event.

"I feel it is a sport which enables people from any background to have fun. It is particularly special to people who can't walk into a field and run around. It allows people in wheelchairs (and others not too steady on their feet) to see the countryside from a different height and to choose where they go and at what speed. Driving people are also a very friendly bunch and always seem willing to help each other. I am especially grateful to our own pony Red Rascal, who introduced me to driving, and the Stella Hancock Group, without whom none of this story could have been told."

* * *

"I first came to hear of the West Horsley Driving Group while in a swimming pool," recalls Elizabeth Tyas. "My daughters were members of the Spartan Swimming Club and a fellow member was Pam Le Mottee. We had just bought Red Rascal, a little section A ride and drive pony, and were busy showing Pam some photographs one day when she began to tell us about her driving group.

"Some time later Stella Hancock died and the group, now renamed the Stella Hancock Group, sent out a request for people to come along and help. With Pam's encouragement I went along with a friend, Helen Pritchard, and although apprehensive because I didn't really know what was in store, soon realised that my fears were unfounded. I was warmly welcomed and made to feel very useful. I also soon made a host of new stalwart friends.

"After about a year of helping and grooming, I was given the chance to further my driving education and, as I had heard John Parker speaking at a BDS event and thoroughly enjoyed listening to him, I chose to attend a driving course at his stables in Wingfield. I returned bursting with enthusiasm and soon afterwards began helping as an AB whip.

"That same year, 1989, I was the AB whip for my daughter Lindsey at the 25th BDS Show at Smith's Lawn, where she won a very memorable first prize and a beautiful commemorative bronze of a horse's head.

"Since then our pony Red Rascal has been approved as an RDA pony and has given, and is still giving, pleasure to so many people. We have driven in the forest, taken part in musical drives, inter-regional competitions and, in 1993, supplied the wedding turnout for two of our members who were married and celebrated later with a party at Hillside.

"Joining the Stella Hancock Group has opened many doors for me and our whole family is now involved. I've met many dear and loyal friends and I think my fondest memories must be of 1990 when Lindsey won her Harpers and Queen's Scholarship and our great friend Carol Lee won the Stella Hancock Scholarship. I was lucky enough to accompany her when she took up her scholarship at John Parker's and achieved her ambition of driving a pair. She did it in style, driving two of John's Hungarian horses.

"My only regret is that I didn't join the group earlier as, although I spoke to Stella on the telephone, I never met the legendary lady."

*   *   *

Ponies can sometimes have a remedial effect on children in rather unexpected circumstances as in the case of eleven years old Goran Dubravac. He was a badly shell shocked young Bosnian boy who had flown to England with his pregnant mother in 1994, leaving his father and other members of his family behind in war torn Sarajevo.

After a while he went to West Hill School in Leatherhead, where many of the pupils have various learning difficulties and some are also physically disabled. He was still very homesick and found difficulty in making friends because he only understood a few words of English.

Children can often play happily together even when there are language barriers, but Goran was a loner and still badly scarred mentally by all he had been through in Bosnia. The teachers found difficulty in communicating with him and he became more and more withdrawn and unwilling to take an interest in anything the other pupils were doing.

When some of the junior pupils were taken for riding lessons with the RDA's Horsley Group on Tuesday afternoons, he agreed rather reluctantly to go with them, but when he saw a pony for the first time he was terrified. He was so frightened he couldn't be persuaded to go near enough to even touch one and ran off screaming when asked to do so.

According to Sonia Windsor, who organised the riding lessons, Goran seemed to have a phobia about all animals. "Many children have been nervous or hesitant to begin with, but this young boy was completely terrified and we began to think that he was going to be our first real failure", she admitted.

They fetched Star, a 20 year old New Forest cross, who had taught many disabled children to ride and was a great favourite with all the school's pupils. Star just stood there for more than half an hour, waiting patiently while Goran's schoolfriends encouraged him to go up to the pony. The boy eventually took what seemed like a very deep breath and allowed one of the instructors to lift him into the saddle.

Star didn't move until Goran's feet were safely in the stirrups and then with the boy holding on grimly to the helpers on either side, set off slowly round the indoor arena of the riding school. Goran still couldn't be persuaded to touch Star, but he had overcome the first hurdle.

He returned the following week, but still wouldn't approach Star and it was 20 minutes before he would do so and let himself be helped into the saddle. This time, however, he began to relax a little as the pony walked slowly round and even managed a grin as the lesson came to an end.

On the third week Goran was the first to leave the school's minibus and ran into the riding school calling for Star by name. The little bay pony was saddled up ready for the lesson and this time Goran stood at his head, stroking his nose and patting him, before being helped into the saddle. Pony and rider were again led round the indoor school, but before the end of the afternoon Goran insisted on taking hold of the reins himself and guided Star unaided. When he did so everyone clapped and cheered and Goran beamed with delight.

He was obviously enjoying himself for the first time since his arrival in England. When the children were back at school he began behaving like a different boy and seemed anxious not to do anything which might have prevented his Tuesday visits to Star. Within a short time he had learned to trot and ride unaided and by the end of the school term had progressed enough to take the Riding for the Disabled Grade I test and pass with flying colours. Several of the instructors and helpers had tears in their eyes as the young Bosnian boy received his award.

He'd not only shown great courage in conquering his fear of ponies, but was obviously enjoying life again and his English had improved enough for him to talk to Star as a friend. Many children have conquered a fear of ponies and learned to enjoy riding, but in Goran's case a pony had also enabled him to forget.

Chapter Nineteen
Special Events

During the 25 years following the launch of the West Horsley Group of the RDA there have been many highlights and days to remember. Dreams have been realised, ambitions achieved and hundreds of disabled people, young and old, given the chance to experience the excitement of special occasions and do things they had never thought possible.

The Variety Club of Great Britain is dedicated to helping underprivileged and handicapped children and in 1974 donated five portable tack rooms to the RDA. The first of these was given to the West Horsley and erected at Wyvenhoe, where it was officially received by Princess Anne on October 23rd 1974. An excited group of children and helpers gathered to await the arrival of the Princess, who flew by helicopter from London and landed in a nearby field. A short car journey brought her to Wyvenhoe, where she was greeted by a group of handicapped riders who formed a 'Guard of Honour'. In the excitement, one small boy lost a tooth which caused a good deal of blood and accompanying screams. Unperturbed, the Princess asked to see the tooth, which was then proudly shown to everyone.

In the indoor school the Princess watched a dressage display by Eugenia – paralysed from the waist down as a result of polio – followed by a working ride.

Twenty two children gave an impressive demonstration of riding with and without stirrups and reins, work on the lunge, trotting over poles and cavaletti, and exercises. The Princess then presented all of the riders with a rosette and spoke to each of the helpers. A special presentation was made to Sue Parker's Merrylegs, who at the age of 25 had raised more than £100 for the group with appearances at local fêtes and gymkhanas.

Royal patronage has played an important part in the development of the RDA, in particular the support of the Princess Royal who, as Patron and now President, has shown a genuine and sustained interest in the association's activities. On a number of occasions competition success for West Horsley riders has been crowned by the presentation of their prize by the Princess and her appearance always creates great excitement. In 1979 West Horsley members Sheila Ingram and Peggy Broad met the Princess at Ascot racecourse, where Her Royal Highness spoke to pony and donkey drivers belonging to RDA groups in the south of England.

The Royal Windsor Horse Show has been the scene of several past West Horsley triumphs in the fancy dress class which is held for invited disabled groups. The number of children able to participate from each group depended on the theme, the number of available ponies and support of parents who were needed to help with costumes and so on. Wyvenhoe ponies were often used as privately owned ponies, although of finer quality, were unused to disabled riders. The children themselves were much more confident on familiar animals and tended to 'freeze' when mounted on a strange pony.

The theme of Snow White and the Seven Dwarfs required a great deal of organisation. The dwarfs had to be tied together so that none got lost, but all the hard work was rewarded with first prize which was presented by Princess Anne. The children always enjoyed dressing up and the excitement of the show. The Sad and Happy Clowns also took first prize one year and Worzel Gummidge accompanied by Aunt Sally upheld the honour of the group by taking second place.

The Variety Club has provided continual support. Eight children from the Park School and Hatchford Park represented the West Horsley at a Variety Club lunch and Radio One roadshow at the Savoy Hotel in London in June 1979, for children who had benefited from the club's fund raising. The journey to London was undertaken in the Park School's new Sunshine coach and after a 'bangers and mash' lunch the children met many of the famous disc jockeys, returning to Surrey with a host of autographs and happy memories of a special day.

Thanks again to the Variety Club, the Tuesday ride became television stars when the West Horsley was asked to take part in filming for the BBC television programme Superstars. Filming took place outside term time but nevertheless Sybil Atherton managed to gather together children and helpers for the day. In true filming tradition, however, there were plenty of problems and delays and by the time the film crew were ready it was too dark to continue. Undeterred everyone returned the next day and the results were seen by millions of viewers.

The importance of publicity for the RDA was not lost on Stella Hancock, who knew the value of media exposure. The Lord Mayor's Show is an enormous pageant that has passed through the streets of the City of London on the day of the Lord Mayor's installation for the past 400 years and is watched by half a million people along the route and another four million on television. As well as the motorised floats, more than 100 horses are ridden or driven in the parade, and in 1984, thanks to the efforts of Stella Hancock, four of the West Horsley's disabled drivers were among the participants.

The ponies – Justin, Christopher Robin, Star and Miss Muffitt – spent the night before the show in the Royal Mews at Buckingham Palace in the company of 32 large Royal carriage horses who also took part. Early in the morning the four turnouts, accompanied by the Royal horses and a police escort, made their way along the Mall and through Horse Guards Arch, to the Guildhall Yard near the Mansion House, where they joined the small group to which they had been assigned, ready to take their place at the end of the procession as it passed.

Neil Portsmouth, who drove Christopher Robin, recalls the unforgettable experience of leaving the quiet side street to be met by the cheering crowds. "It was one of those occasions that is very hard to describe," he says, "but it must be similar to the feeling that footballers experience as they come out onto the pitch at Wembley for the Cup Final. There is literally a wall of sound and the noise of the crowds cheering was amazing."

In spite of the roar of the crowd the ponies behaved perfectly. The only problem occurred when the vehicle drive by Millie Millington suffered a puncture soon after setting off, which was quickly dealt with by one of the BHS Horse Driving Trials members following behind on foot. "He pulled the tube clear," recalls Millie, "and then had to remove the tyre as well. So we did most of the journey over London's cobbles on the rim of the wheel. Ouch!" The discomfort did nothing to diminish the excitement of the occasion, which the drivers knew was something that few people are ever lucky enough to experience.

Felicity Andrews particularly remembers leaving the Royal Mews with a police escort. Her pony Star was not entirely traffic proof and while circling Queen Victoria's memorial a taxi driver who tried to cut in front of them received a blow from a driving whip across his bonnet.

Paul de Vere drove Justin, accompanied by Jack Burrill. "It was great fun," Paul recalls, "and Justin looked a real show winner with his jet black shiny coat and long flowing mane as we trotted through the streets of London. Jack and I were dressed in our best suits and bowler hats and we felt like VIPs as the crowds thronged the barriers to wave at the procession. We trotted along behind a carriage pulled by a team of Shires. It was from one of the oldest breweries in London and when we pulled in for lunch the two coachmen climbed down and saw us parked beside them. 'Well, it's Jack and young Justin, isn't it?' one of them said. 'Here's a beer for you and one for your mate'. It certainly washed our pork pies down well."

The Lord Mayor's Show might have been considered by most people to be the ultimate achievement, but not Stella Hancock. Always looking for new challenges for her Ben Hurs, she used people from all over the country as sounding boards for her numerous ideas. In 1986, when Britain hosted the World Four-in-Hand Championships at Ascot,

Stella's ambitious plan was to produce a musical drive to show the world what the handicapped could do. Fourteen turnouts from nine groups around the country were included and plans of the drive were sent to the drivers involved, who then practised within their own groups. The first full rehearsal tool place at Ascot on the morning of the first demonstration and unbelievably everything simply slotted into place.

"We took a risk," admitted Stella Hancock afterwards, "and everyone responded magnificently. The key was to keep the drive simple and effective as there had never been so many in the ring all at once. The key performers were the leading turnout – Avril Lewis's outstanding grey pony Mork driven by Lesley Blaze from the West Horsley group – who set the tempo and led the way. Other seasoned campaigners who had performed in public before and can cope with the euphoric atmosphere and razzamataz were spaced out in the drive, allowing those who had never had this sort of experience to be well supported. Much to our relief it worked – and worked well."

The two musical drives were performed without a hitch and proved to people from different parts of the world that handicapped drivers could match the able bodied for skill. The performances attracted considerable interest, not only from spectators but also the top drivers who were impressed by the ability of the disabled whips. Of the many tributes which Stella Hancock received after the event, Ascot's clerk of the course Captain Nicky Beaumont described it as the 'Drive of the Century'. It was yet another triumph for the driving for the disabled movement and Stella Hancock's Ben Hurs.

The reputation of the West Horsley driving group had resulted in the chance to join in another demonstration during the previous year, when four of the group's drivers were invited to take part in a musical drive at the Olympia Christmas Show to celebrate the 21st anniversary of Riding for the Disabled. As Neil Portsmouth explains, the occasion realised one of his childhood dreams. "One day I told Stella that on a visit to Olympia as a child I had said, 'I'll be down there in the arena one day.' A few months later she asked me if I would like to take part in a musical drive at the show and so, thanks to Stella, I achieved another of my ambitions."

Paul de Vere also took part in the musical drive at Olympia, driving Valentine Cadell's large pony Miss Muffitt. "Valentine constantly had to remind me when driving in the dressage arena at home not to fall in around the corners," Paul remembers, "and I could hear her advice ringing in my ears when we entered the arena at Olympia. It was bedecked with little Christmas trees in green tubs and all sorts of Christmas paraphernalia. Miss Muffitt was powerful and with her long stride we were soon zipping round with the music. I remembered to get into my corners so well that the outside wheel of the carriage clipped one of the Christmas trees and sent it spinning through the air. It landed on its side amongst all the other glitter but luckily Miss Muffitt didn't even flinch. Valentine just laughed and we finished the drive perfectly in time with the music."

Further appearances at major events such as the Metropolitan Police Show at Imber Court brought the skill of the West Horsley drivers to a wider audience and three days after the Lord Mayor's Show they performed their musical drive in front of Princess Anne and more than 300 delegates at the National RDA Conference at Stoneleigh. Stalwart helper Sybilla McCann had to fill in for one of the disabled drivers and not only took part in the musical drive but drove from a wheelchair. "There was no way you could say 'no' to Stella," she recalls with a smile.

Chapter Twenty
Jubilee Celebrations

The visit by HRH the Princess Royal to the Stella Hancock Group at Hillside Manor Farm, West Horsley, on Tuesday, May 24th 1994, was undoubtedly the highlight of the Jubilee Celebrations. She arrived by helicopter to be received by the Lord Lieutenant for Surrey, Mr Richard Thornton, OBE JP. After being introduced to important local dignitaries and officials of the RDA, who included the Chairman, Elizabeth Dendy MBE, and being presented with a posy by Lisa Kup-Ferroth, she met the owners of Hillside Manor Farm, Mr and Mrs Stephen Larkin, and had an opportunity to talk to representatives of the West Horsley Riding Group and the Stella Hancock Driving Group.

The Princess Royal showed considerable interest in the lesson being given to five disabled drivers, and watched a very impressive musical drive by four members of the Driving Group, which had been specially arranged for the occasion. She then presented rosettes to a number of disabled riders and drivers and, before leaving, unveiled a plaque to formerly open the new pony premises. It was a visit which brought a tremendous amount of pleasure to everyone associated with riding and driving for the disabled in the area.

The Riding Group benefited very considerably by John Vandeleur-Boorer's involvement with the National Trust and was able to use the delightful accommodation at Polesden Lacey for a variety of events, as well as committee meetings. The National Trust also gave permission for a special Jubilee event to be held there during the annual fortnight when open air plays and an opera take place. Apart from the beautiful setting, the RDA also had the added advantage of being able to use the marquees which had been erected for the special activities organised by the Trust.

The RDA function included a dinner, musical entertainment, a wine tasting and a quite remarkable demonstration by Phillipa Verey, who was born without arms. It showed what can be achieved through determination and nerve in overcoming what most people would look upon as almost impossible odds.

Like many other young girls, Phillipa dreamed of working with horses. She learned to ride and look after horses until she was proficient enough to run her own yard and take in liveries. She also learned to drive a horse box.

Her ridden demonstration showed dressage movements to medium level and the high standard of competence horse and rider had already achieved. Phillipa competes successfully in affiliated dressage classes at national level and has already proved her undoubted talent as an instructor and as a rider.

It was, however, the next part of the demonstration which showed the extent with which she has overcome her disability. Everyone thought that putting a saddle and bridle on a horse must be one task Phillipa couldn't accomplish on her own. How wrong they were.

She took the saddle and bridle to the horse herself, using her chin against her shoulder to carry first of all a chair on which the equipment was to be placed and then the various items of tack she needed. She used her feet to put the bridle in place, doing up the buckles with her toes. Then, after putting the numnah on the horse's back, again used her toes to swing the saddle in place and do up the girths. Within a few minutes she had her horse tacked up, with everything in place and fitting perfectly.

Little wonder that the whole evening was such a success and Phillipa's amazing demonstration of grit, determination and ability helped raise a considerable sum for RDA funds.

Chapter Twenty-One
Progress with International Driving Trials

Dressage for disabled riders is already a World Championship sport, but the International Carriage Driving Trial which took place at Hartpury College, Gloucester, from July 21st to the 24th at the same time as the 1994 World Dressage Championship for Disabled Riders, may also have far reaching effects.

Carriage driving enables many disabled people to compete at a level which is close to the standard achieved by the majority of able bodied drivers. In some cases they even do better. This was evident at Hartpury, where everything was done to make it a tough and thrilling event, with very solid, free flowing hazards on the cross country, which had been designed and built by Tishie Roberts, the well-known international course builder. His aim was to test each driver's skill and courage, without running the risk of serious injury and he succeeded in doing so beyond everyone's hopes and expectations.

The British team for the event was chosen early in February and members of the Stella Hancock Driving Group were 'cock a hoop' when a telephone call revealed that two of their members, Judi Ralls and Lindsey Tyas, had been chosen for the team of four competitors to represent Britain. The others were Dilly Ahern from the West Somerset Carriage Driving Group and Jane O'Neill, a member of the Willows Carriage Driving Group. To add to the excitement Christine David, another of Stella Hancock's famous 'Ben Hurs', had been selected as the British team's reserve driver. Judi Ralls, Lindsey Tyas and Christine David had all finished in the first five at the trials held at Hartpury the previous summer.

Caroline Douglas took them all under her wing for several weeks' intensive instruction, which would have done credit to any British driving team. Everyone took the training very seriously and accepted the fact that they were being worked close to the limit as a sign of their determination not to let the British team down. Slowly their dressage improved and they learned how to 'read' each hazard on a cross country, in order to chose the quickest and safest route, as well as the other aspects to look out for when 'walking' the course on their Honda Trikes.

The team members also found Caroline's advice on feeding invaluable, so that the ponies peaked at just the right time. Because of the very hot weather, the grey gelding Shandy, one of the older but very experienced ponies, was given a course of electrolytes during the weeks leading up to the event, to ensure that he was at his best.

Sunday, July 17th, was a brilliantly sunny day. Everything had been packed, checked and double checked and the team spirit was very much in evidence when Brenda May arrived at Crondall to help Nick and Judi Ralls to load up. Shandy looked immaculate in his best travelling rugs, boots and bandages and showed signs of excitement as he peered over his stable door to watch the preparations. He'd already become an old hand at driving trials, having also competed with the Ralls when they lived in Germany and has a German passport to prove it.

Their three horse trailer was loaded to the gunnels with their best driving harness, a set of exercise harness, wet weather gear, enough food for Shandy to last a week, lamps, cleaning material, paint and Judi's Honda Trike, which they just managed to squeeze in under their driving vehicle.

Shandy was eventually loaded into the trailer and with the Rall's two large labradors just finding enough space in the car, they set off in high spirits to join the other members of the British team at Hartpury.

They were the first British drivers to arrive and as they set up camp their neighbour, Mo Francis, another disabled driver, provided them with a welcoming cup of tea and with Shandy happily installed in his Woodhouse stable, everyone began to feel quite at home.

In the evening, immediately after supper, a ceremony was held in the main marquee, which enabled competitors and officials to meet and welcome the teams from other countries. The Worshipful Company of Glovers presented a pair of white driving gloves to each team member and with competitors dressed in their team uniforms and anxious to try out their foreign languages, the evening developed into an extremely colourful and noisy affair.

Some of the uniforms were quite striking. The Germans looked very macho; the Americans wore their stars and stripes; the Swedish were in blue and yellow; the single entry from Canada sported a maple leaf and, to cap it all, the Argentinian driver wore a dashing cloak and a Spanish hat. The atmosphere was quite electric and the evening seemed to set the pace for the rest of the week.

The Tyas family arrived the next day with their pony Red Rascal, who was stabled alongside Shandy. There were a few last minute panics in the British team when a broken spring on one of the carts had to be repaired and there were fears among many of the competitors that their ponies might not have experienced a water hazard. Fortunately this fear proved to be unfounded and all the ponies coped with the water very well.

The alarm clocks were set for 4.15am on the Thursday morning to make sure that Judi and Brenda had their ponies ready for the Presentation at 8am. The ponies were groomed and given their breakfasts at

6.30am and then harnessed up and put to in time to be walked gently down to the Presentation Box for the inspection. Then it was on to the dressage arena, where tests were due to start about half an hour later.

Judi and Shandy didn't do a very good dressage, partly due to nerves, but Lindsey and Red made up for it with a nice accurate test and a score of 44.3, which, when added to Dilly Ahern's mark of 41.0 as only the best two from each team counted, put the British team in second place behind the Germans.

The cones competition was next and the test Andrew Counsell had set drove very well. Everyone suppressed the urge to canter and enjoyed driving such a flowing course after the tension of the dressage. The ebullient German, Hans Lehrter, was the winner and having also won the individual dressage with a score of 39.9 took the overnight lead, but Dilly was second in the cones phase, with Judi placed third. At the party that evening Hans Lehrter was heard to remark with a great deal of glee "tomorrow we are fighting."

The afternoon had been taken up with a rather grand Olympic style opening ceremony, with the grandstand filled with supporters and helpers and each team followed their country's flag into the main arena. The ringside seats were also packed with members of the public and visitors from RDA Groups, some of whom had travelled long distances to be present. They were not disappointed, with riders and drivers representing a total of 15 countries from many parts of the world.

Music was provided by the band of the Royal Electrical and Mechanical Engineers (R.E.M.E.) and those taking part in the afternoon's entertainment included a team of riders from the West Midland Police Mounted Branch; the well-known Lloyds Bank black stallion, Downlands Cancara; the Prince Philip Cup team from the North Warwickshire branch of the Pony Club; the Fife Riding Club Quadrille and a display of British native breeds, which included two Shetlands ridden by Alison and John Tyas. The highlight of the afternoon was the arrival of HRH the Princess Royal riding in one of the Queen's carriages from the Royal Mews. The royal horses were stabled overnight next to Shandy and Red, which provided an aura of grandeur which they hadn't previously experienced.

Friday was cross-country day, which all the competitors had been looking forward to with a mixture of excitement and anticipation. Everyone had 'walked' each hazard several times and debated and argued with the other team members about the best way to tackle them. There was a general feeling of relief when the officials decided to relax the rule which insisted on each pony having two pairs of reins, one for the disabled driver and the other for the accompanying able bodied whip.

The British team's grooms were also allowed to ride on the back steps of their driving vehicles. This enabled them to give the vehicles more stability going through the hazards, by leaning out and transferring their weight from side to side when going round corners at speed.

The German and American teams, like the British, were used to competing at national and international level in their own countries, which did give them an edge. The hazards had been built by Tishie Roberts with the aid of some fine timber provided by Tilhill Economic Forestry, whose managing director Andrew Jennings was a very generous supporter of the event. The hazards were quite magnificent, very solid, with a choice of long or short routes and demanding accurate driving by those determined to make fast times.

The ponies sensed that it was cross-country day as soon as their boots were taped on and their tails were bandaged up and they could see their drivers putting on back protectors and crash helmets. There was just enough time for a quick warm up in a quiet corner before it was down to the start, the stop watches were checked and the green cards were tucked safely into the grooms' bibs ready for the off.

Section A was a short sharp pipe opener, which was enough to get the adrenalin going, but competitors had to be careful not to complete the section too quickly, so that they arrived at the finish too early and incurred penalty points. Section B was a one kilometre walk on a long rein around a cricket pitch, which would have made a fine dressage arena, but the real fun started at Section E. The drivers experienced probably the best set of hazards anyone had encountered and those who were bold enough to tackle some of the faster routes and got away with it, reaped the benefit with some good scores.

At the end of a very exciting competition, the American driver Mary Grey was the first individual, but there was a British element to her win, because she had been driving Merlin, a lovely 17 years old pony belonging to Sue Riches, the chairman of the RDA Driving Committee. Because of the distances involved a number of the overseas competitors had been loaned ponies for the event. Second place went to Karl-Bernd Kaesgen of Germany.

The German driver Heiner Lehrter, who'd been in the lead after the first day, was sadly eliminated when in his exuberance he missed a turning flag. Even so, his times through the hazards were slower than those of Dilly Ahern, the Somerset farmer's wife, who finished third with 97.0 points, and Judi Ralls, who finished fourth on 102.6, enabling the British team to take second place, only half a point behind the German team, with the Americans placed third. The result could not have been closer.

It was, however, a competition when there were no real losers and George France, a member of the Canadian team, summed up everyone's feelings when he said: "We are all winners in every sense, because we all accomplished the course. We came to Hartpury to prove it could be done and to make the event a great success and that's what we did". Writing in the Daily Telegraph, Alan Smith made the point that the drivers had made no concession to their disabilities. "They were as highly competitive as anyone will be at the World Equestrian Games in The Hague next week", he wrote.

The final line up for the presentation was very impressive and would have done justice to any World Championship. So would the commentary given by Andrew Cowdery, another well-known disabled driver, as the competitors came forward to receive their rosettes and prizes.

The closing ceremony, at the conclusion of the World Dressage Championships, ended in a spectacular fireworks display, with HARTPURY 1994 depicted in the flames. This was followed by a final party, where all the competitors were able to say their farewells and look forward to their next meeting. Everyone was invited to attend the National Riding for the Disabled Conference in November to receive their trophies officially from HRH the Princess Royal. Following the official visit which the Princess Royal had paid to West Horsley on May 24th, this came as a fitting end to a spectacular year for the Stella Hancock Driving Group.

Chapter Twenty-Two
Driving into the Future

The disabled driving movement is still developing and has come a long way since Prince Philip's suggestion that driving may be a suitable activity for people with disabilities. Care has been taken that the progress has been sensible and safe and that the growing number of drivers who want to compete can get their thrills without the risk of unnecessary spills.

There is no doubt, however, that the ability that some disabled drivers now have to compete at a high level, and even take on able bodied whips on occasions, is a tremendous encouragement to those who are just starting and now realise the opportunities open to them. The courage and skill of those at the top has proved a tremendous catalyst towards continuous progress and those responsible for running the disabled drivers movement have, for the most part, responded well to the challenge.

The course at Hartpury, for example, for the International Driving Trials held there in July 1994, was up to world standards, according to Ron Hancock, the technical delegate, apart from the overall distance which had been reduced to seven kilometres, mostly through the hazard section, because of the very hot weather. All the competitors said that they enjoyed themselves immensely and welcomed the opportunity of taking part in an event which taxed their stamina and skill.

This thought was obviously in many people's minds when they attended the 1995 RDA Driving Conference, held at the King's Bush Centre at Godmanchester, Huntington, on March 1st and 2nd. The Stella Hancock Group was particularly well represented and included Felicity Andrews, Sheila Caley, Christine David, Hella De Vere and Paul De Vere, Ron Hancock, Paul Hanson, Brenda May, Sybella McCann, Beverley Melstrom, Gail Piprose, Neil Portsmouth, Dave and Helen Pritchard, Judi Ralls, Paul, Elizabeth and Lindsey Tyas and David Washbourne.

All the 300 delegates during the two days showed an enthusiasm and willingness to take positive action to improve the sport, which helped to make the Conference such an outstanding success. For example, a growing number of drivers wanted to try driving a four wheeler and many of them made their wishes known in the strongest terms. So much so that they managed to overcome the views formerly held by many that four wheelers were not suitable for disabled drivers. Fifty or so of them had already tried driving one, following the design competition for two and four wheelers sponsored in 1984 by the Worshipful Company of Coach Makers and Coachharness Makers. They were all in favour of bringing in four wheel vehicles and described their experience of driving them as "Superb! Very much more comfortable than two wheelers."

The theme for the Conference was 'Driving into the Future', which proved an excellent choice. The morning of the first day was taken up with demonstrations and instruction on cones driving, particularly for people with impaired vision, teaching skills and the correct way of presenting a wheelchair to a vehicle, and closed with a very interesting talk by Annalisa Barrelet, a leading veterinary surgeon. The afternoon session included talks on safety, the best way to assess the ability of able bodied whips and an informal discussion with regional driving representatives. The chairman of the British Driving Society, Peter Nichols, was the guest speaker at the dinner that evening.

The second day began with a talk on 'Starting to Drive', followed by discussions on roll bars, one pair of reins, four wheeled vehicles and presenting the whip in a wheelchair before 'putting to'. Members of the Stella Hancock Group, Neil Portsmouth and Paul Hanson, as well as Ron Hancock, who represents the RDA on the International Paralympic Equestrian Committee, were members of the panel during a general discussion on driving and in the afternoon delegates were able to inspect and drive the latest four wheel vehicles and get special advice on the vital importance of the balance of two wheelers.

The Conference ended with a musical drive by members of the Stella Hancock Group, which was so well received that they were invited to perform at the Royal Agricultural Show at Stoneleigh in July.

As a member of the International Paralympic Equestrian Committee, Ron Hancock has been involved in writing some special rules for disabled drivers which are as close as possible to the FEI rules governing international driving trials. If the Committee's new rules are accepted, disabled driving will become a paralympic sport, with World Championships being held during the intervening years. How Stella Hancock would have approved! Her 'Ben Hurs' are at last to be given a chance to show just how good they can be at overcoming their disabilities and at being shining examples of courage, determination, dedication and skill.

There is no doubt that the lift being given to disabled driving at the top end of the sport will also permeate throughout the disabled driving movement and eventually benefit everyone, down to the newest recruit to driving. Ron Hancock emphasised, however, that RDA drivers cover a wide spectrum of disabilities and, of course, ages. While it is important to be continually trying to raise standards at the top competitive level and provide fresh challenges for those seeking them, it must never be overlooked that the majority of the regulars and learners drive just for the sheer fun of doing so and don't have any competitive ambitions.

Chapter Twenty-Three
The Future

When Major John Vandeleur-Boorer took over as chairman of the West Horsley A, B and C groups in March 1990, he inherited an organisation which he described as, "financially creaky but run by wonderful, devoted people". His job as administrator of Polesden Lacey, one of the National Trust's busiest properties, left him little time to become actively involved in the day to day running of the groups, but he did bring a valuable fresh pair of eyes to the problems of administration, soon simplified by the merger of the three riding groups. An attempt to reunite the riding and driving groups was unsuccessful, however, and the two remain separate organisations.

Although his wife Elizabeth had previously been involved with the groups as a helper he had little knowledge of the RDA, but a visit to one of the riding sessions at Wyvenhoe convinced him of the benefits it offered to handicapped people. He soon realised that the target of £3,000 to cover the annual costs was totally inadequate. "The arrangement with Wyvenhoe had not been reviewed for seven years," he explained, "and the riding school was way out of pocket. They had been very kind and generous but a more realistic approach was needed. We duly revised the charges and as a result had to increase the target of our fund raising to £7,000."

Continued support from local organisations and an increase in fund raising efforts have resulted in an improvement in the financial situation, which now appears to be increasingly healthy. However, as Wyvenhoe is now looking to liveries as a more profitable side of their business, the riding school horses and ponies are not being replaced when they reach retirement age. If Wyvenhoe is lost, this could jeopardise the Horsley operation and the loss of their weekly riding lesson would be a severe blow to the disabled adults and children to whom it means freedom and fun. It would be ironic if the wheel turns full circle and the riding group has again to rely on privately owned ponies and the generosity of individuals prepared to make available their own indoor schools and land.

John Vandeleur-Boorer resigned as chairman when he left the district in the autumn of 1994 on retiring from the National Trust. His place has been taken by Colin Wenborn, who is also the Group's treasurer and his highly constructive, enthusiastic and businesslike approach is helping to steer the Horsley Group successfully into the next century.

It is comforting to know that the Driving Group now has a permanent base at Hillside Manor Farm, a nucleus of keen disabled whips and able bodied drivers with reliable ponies, providing a solid foundation for the future. There will always be aspects of the Group's activities, like the training of new helpers, which will need to be constantly reviewed, but the commitment and determination is already there to overcome problems as they arise.

It is, however, this commitment and enthusiasm on the part of everyone involved with the riding and driving activities, which will ensure that the efforts and successes of the past 25 years will prove to be just the first chapters in the search for fun and freedom and not the whole story.

Appendix

A REVIEW OF IMPORTANT EVENTS IN THE GROUP'S HISTORY

1969   The inaugural meeting was held at Hillside Farm, West Horsley, on November 26th. The first committee was formed and consisted of Gillian Drew (Secretary), Barron Holyroyd (Treasurer), Ron and Stella Hancock, Anne Creswell, Sue Parker, Carol Riley (Helpers Organiser), Rachel Wilson (Principal Instructor), John Collier, Terry Thompson, Ted Leahy (Bridleways-Saddlery Advisor), Miss M. Price (Medical Liaison Officer), Gilly Blake, Betty Crutchley and Christine Isaac.

First donations received of £50 from the Billy Butlin Charity Trust and the Surrey County Playing Fields Association.

On December 10th the first committee meeting was held and Ron Hancock was appointed Chairman, with Sue Parker as Vice-Chairman and Stella Hancock as Public Relations Officer. Carolyn Edwards-Jones was welcomed as the Group's first physiotherapist.

1970   Although there hadn't been any response to the approaches made to Sendhurst Grange and Hatchford Park, by February a number of individual children were keen to begin riding. The first ride took place on May 5th with Paul Creswell and four children from Hatchford Park.

The Surrey County Playing Fields Association offered financial assistance and eight pupils were riding regularly by September.

1971   A class started in May for 12 mentally handicapped adolescents from Pond Meadow and in September a Thursday morning class began for private children.

The first annual general meeting of the West Horsley Riding for the Disabled Group was held in November and the Secretary reported that 247 rides had taken place since May 1970 and 10 members of the group had passed the Stage 1 proficiency test and 8 had passed Stage 2.

1972   Progress continued and throughout the year 19 children were riding on a regular basis at Hillside Farm.

1973 It was decided that the facilities at Hillside Farm were no longer sufficient to deal with the growing demand for lessons and June Childs offered the use of the Wyvenhoe Riding Centre indoor school and ponies for all the rides, except for those on Thursday morning. All the rides would be under the direction of Gilly Blake, Jean Bishop and Carol Riley, who would act as organisers.

Riding was included in the curriculum at Hatchford Park.

Nigel Pegg, a seven year old mongol boy, left the Group to ride with able bodied children. Another pupil, Gill McKenzie from Pond Meadow, won the National RDA painting competition.

Stella Hancock took over as Secretary.

1974 The Group had 56 regular riders and gave 1874 rides. Children from Hatchford Park rode on Tuesday mornings; there were four sessions on Thursday mornings for adolescents from Pond Meadow and children from other special schools in the area, including one from the Blind School in Leatherhead.

HRH Princess Anne opened the new tack room presented to the Group by the Variety Club of Great Britain.

Stable management lessons were started.

1975 The Group had 74 regular riders. Ron Hancock retired as Chairman and was succeeded by Ted Leahy. The Thursday morning sessions were merged. The Group joined in the BBC's Blue Peter Appeal in aid of the RDA by collecting material and old clothes.

1976 After a visit to the Sandhurst Driving for the Disabled Group by Felicity Andrews, Sarah Garnett and Stella Hancock had discussions with Nancy Pethick, it was decided to form a West Horsley Driving for the Disabled Group.

Stella Hancock took over as Organiser following Sue Parker's resignation and the Tuesday ride was extended to cater for the waiting list.

The Group was invited to take part in the RDA sponsored showjumping at Goodwood and Samantha Gill was the winner.

1977 The inaugural meeting of the Driving Group took place in March and driving started in May with four regular drivers having lessons on Wednesday afternoons.

Pam Phillips, one of the disabled riders, was elected to the Group Committee and the best 24 riders from Lockwood left the Group to form a new ride at Wyvenhoe which didn't require helpers.

1978 Evening rides were started for disabled adults from The Grange who were working during the day. The Driving Group was visited by Sally Raw, the Chairman of the RDA Driving Committee.

A new driving vehicle capable of carrying a wheelchair and a passenger was approved. It had been designed by Jack Burrill and built by John Wilks.

The Driving Group was invited to send two turnouts and drivers to give a demonstration at the National Conference at Stoneleigh.

Tim Buckley, a Riding Group pupil, finished third in the RDA Prix Caprilli held at Hever Castle.

An approach was made by the King George V Hospital for riding to be provided for some of the long stay patients in the hospital's special unit. This led to the formation of the Shackleford Group.

The West Horsley Group took part in the BBC's filming of Superstars for the Variety Club of Great Britain.

A new, self-financing ride was started for pupils at the Park School in Woking.

1979   Rides were now being held each week on Tuesday, Wednesday, Thursday and Friday and on each occasion pupils were asked to contribute 50p towards the cost.

Four of the Group's riders took part in the Pony Club's Golden Jubilee Parade.

Jill Berliand succeeded Ted Leahy as Chairman and Anne Creswell and Sue Parker retire from the main committee.

Members of the Group win the ridden fancy dress event at the Royal Windsor Show and also take third place in the driven section.

Crawford Simpson, a mentally handicapped rider, passed the British Horse Society Riding and Road Safety Award.

Residents from Dorincourt, in Leatherhead, which is part of the Queen Elizabeth Foundation for the Disabled, join the West Horsley Group.

Eight of the Group's members were invited by the Variety Club of Great Britain to attend the Radio 1 Tribute Lunch at London's Savoy Hotel.

1980   The West Horsley Group was divided into four sections, each with an organiser and secretary. Section A looked after the Tuesday rides; Section B the Wednesday evening rides; Section C the other Wednesday, Thursday and Friday morning rides, and Section D dealt with the driving members. There was an overall organiser, secretary and treasurer and the main committee was made up of three representatives from each group.

A donation of nearly £4,000 from the Chiddingfold Farmers Hunt Kennel Fund was placed in a trust fund that the income from it could be used for the benefit of the Group.

The first issue of The Hoofpick, the Group's own newspaper, appeared. Because so many of the riders and helpers are drawn from such a wide area, it was felt that a regular publication was needed to keep everyone in touch with the latest news and views.

A remarkable 2,200 rides were given during 1980 and the Group was presented with the Queen's Silver Jubilee Certificate.

Michael Kelly was the leading winner at Hever Castle and received his prize from Princess Anne.

Felicity Andrews, Stella Hancock and the pony Prince appeared on the BBC's Blue Peter programme.

1981 Six children from Park School attended the first of a series of Summer Camps run by Yvonne Fisk.

The 'Trotting Alone' certificates were adopted and a directive was received from RDA headquarters that all instructors must be approved.

The Driving Group received two very welcome new driving vehicles. The first was a Jubilee Cart, presented by the Bookham and Horsley Rotary Club, and the other was a gift from the George Abbot School in Guildford.

Sheila Ingram won the RDA class at the British Driving Society Show at Smith's Lawn, Windsor.

A driving pony was purchased out of funds donated by the Rotary Club of Bookham and Horsley and name Rotary Albert.

More than 200 people are now involved with the West Horsley RDA Groups.

1982 Sainsburys, the well-known food chain, donated £500 for the purchase of another driving pony called Sunshine.

The Variety Club of Great Britain installed a new tackroom.

Stella Hancock retired as Secretary.

Everyone was saddened by the death of Sheila Ingram, who that year had again been successful at the British Driving Society Show and at the Ride and Drive Championships the following month.

1983 The Driving Group took charge of its own finances.
Prince, a favourite pony with many group members, died.
Wyvenhoe Riding Centre became a livery yard.

1984 Ron and Stella Hancock retire from the Committee.

Pam Phillips becomes the first member of the RDA to pass the Association's Horsemasters Test.

Three Lockwood riders took part in the dressage section at the Mini-Olympics held at Scunthorpe. Leslie Waller, a deaf rider from the Group won the bronze medal.

The new headmaster at Hatchford Park announced that children from his school could only ride out of school hours, which led to the school leaving the Group.

It became obvious that additional finance would be needed if the riding groups were to survive.

1985   Temple Court School sends 14 children to replace the pupils from Hatchford Park.

1986   Patsy Waugh succeeded Jill Berliand as Chairman. Jack Burrill, who had been a great supporter of the Group, moved out of the area to Sussex.

1987   The Driving Group operates separately.
New trustees were appointed for the Chiddingfold Farmers Hunt Kennel Fund.

1988   Temple Court decided to replace riding with home economics on the school's curriculum.
The pupils were replaced by children from Leatherhead's West Hill School.
Stella Hancock died while on holiday in Australia, shortly after giving driving lessons to a group of disabled people there.

1990   Major John Vandeleur-Boorer took over as Chairman.
Barron Holyrod, the Group Treasurer sadly died and his place was taken by Colin Wenborn.
The B Group gave a demonstration at a Vintage Car Rally at Ripley.
A donation of £1,500 was received from the Lady Noel Byron Association.

1991   The A, B and C Groups were re-united under the title of The Horsley Group and the three organisers were retained to look after the Tuesday, Wednesday and Thursday rides.
Two long serving members retired from the Committee. Sybil Atherton retired after 15 years and Paula Stebbings left after 21 years, having been Chief Instructor for 18 years.

1992   Helen Turk retired after spending nearly 20 years as Group Organiser and her place was taken by Carry Kurk. Prue Goodchild also retired from the Committee.
Kimberly-Clarke Europe agreed to sponsor the annual horse show.

1993   The finances of the Group benefited from a Sponsored Keep Fit and a Jazz Evening, both of which were organised by the Leatherhead Round Table.
Ben, Magic and Sinbad, three of the favourite horses at Wyvenhoe Riding Centre, were retired.

1994 The highlight of the year was the visit of HRH The Princess Royal on May 24th to unveil the new tack room, watch instruction and demonstrations and to meet members.

THE WEST HORSLEY DRIVING GROUP

1983 The West Horsley Driving Group decided to take charge of its own finances.

Driving began at the Wyvenhoe Riding Centre.

The Driving Group took part in a demonstration at the Royal Mews for physiotherapists who had come from all parts of the world.

1984 Rehabilitation patients from RAF Chessington joined the Group. A Carriage Competition was held at the Royal Mews in London on April 9th.

West Horsley RDA members performed a musical drive at the National Conference and then, on November 10th, represented the RDA at the Lord Major's Show.

Paul de Vere and Mary Crittall, as Prince Albert and Queen Victoria, took second prize in the Fancy Dress Class at the Royal Windsor Horse Show and third prize at the Surrey County Show.

1985 Paul de Vere and Milly Millington took part in a Sponsored Drive in Windsor Great Park during April.

On May 5th Gill Jones and Paul Hanson drove down the unopened section of the M25 Motorway between Wisley and Leatherhead.

The same month Paul Hanson, dressed as 'Monte', came second in the Fancy Dress Class at Windsor Royal Horse Show.

Four members of the Group took part in the British Driving Society Show at Windsor. All were placed and Milly Millington won driving Sunshine.

Three turnouts from the Group took part in the Wellington Country Fair during July and the following month four performed a musical drive at the Metropolitan Police Show at Imber Court. Four turnouts also took part in the Christmas Show at Olympia.

The first two-day National Driving Conference for RDA Groups took place.

1986 Neil Portsmouth and Milly Millington, driving Star and Mork, took part in a sponsored drive in Richmond Park during March.

Paul Hanson driving Justin won his class at the British Driving Society Show at Smith's Lawn, Windsor, in June.

Five drivers from the Group gave a musical drive demonstration at the World Carriage Driving Championships.

The Group was also chosen to represent the driving side of the RDA and gave a special demonstration at the Christmas Show at Olympia, to mark the 21st Anniversary of the Association.

1987 It was decided that the Driving Group should operate separately from the Riding Group.

Members were successful at the Royal Windsor Show, coming second in the Fancy Dress Class, and at the Surrey County Show at Guildford, winning the Irene Benjamin Award class.

Richard Pitman was the guest speaker at the 10th Anniversary Celebration Dinner.

1988 Members were devastated by the news that Stella Hancock had died in Australia on February 15th and it was decided to rename the Group The Stella Hancock Group in her honour.

Joe Molloy was placed first in his class at the Surrey Area British Driving Society Show on July 31st.

1989 Members of the Group won two of the classes and were placed at the RDA Show at Ascot and the British Driving Society Shows at Windsor and Bookham. They also took part in a musical drive at the Ham Polo Club's Open Day.

1990 The Group took part in a musical drive at the Leatherhead Lions Carnival on June 9th.

At the RDA National Carriage Driving Championships, held at Wimple Hall, Cambridge, there were two entries for the South East team. Apart from being overall winners they were also second and third in the individual placings.

1991 All the Group's entries were placed at the RDA Show at Smith's Lawn, Windsor and at the Bookham BDS Show.

The Group sent three ponies and helpers to the Carriage Building Competition at the Royal Mews on June 21st. The Getaway Four Wheeler, which won, was paraded by the Group at the annual British Driving Society Show at Smith's Lawn.

New premises were built in September and a Fun Day was organised.

1992 The Group won the Condition and Turnout and the Cones classes at the Royal Windsor Horse Show in May.

These successes were followed by the Group being placed second in the RDA Dressage at the RDA Show and first and third in the FEI Dressage.

At the National Driving Competition held at Gatcombe Park the Group's successes included 2nd place in the Individual Dressage; 1st in the Team Dressage and 3rd in the Cones and Hazards. The Group was also runners-up in the Overall Championship.

At the British Driving Society's Show at Bookham members were 1st, 2nd and 3rd in the Showing Class and 1st and 2nd in the Cones.

1993 The Group provided a team of four to represent the South East Region at the One Day Event held at Hartpury College, Gloucestershire. The team ran out overall winners and individual members were placed 1st, 3rd and 5th.

1994 After a very wet start to the driving season members looked forward to the arrival of HRH The Princess Royal on May 24th to unveil a portable harness room and stabling provided by the Lions Club of Leatherhead.

The Princess Royal watched a lesson being given by Caroline Douglas and then saw a faultless Musical Drive performed by members of the Driving Group. The drive almost had to be cancelled when the lead pony went lame the day before. John Lucas offered the use of his pony Puffin, as soon as he heard what had happened, and the pony proved to be quite brilliant. He didn't put a foot wrong, despite a different driver and never having been in the arena, or heard the music.

After presenting special commemorative rosettes to all the drivers and finding time to speak to everyone, The Princess Royal flew off by helicopter to end a marvellous occasion for the Horsley Group.

Judi Ralls and Lindsey Tyas were chosen for the British team taking part in the International Driving Event at Hartpury College, Gloucestershire, in July. The event was run to a high standard and there was fierce competition among the teams. Victory went to the German team by only half a point, with Great Britain in second place.

1995 The Group was asked to do their musical drive at the Driving Conference held at Cambridge in March. Following this they were invited to do a similar musical drive at the Royal Show on July 6th in the new arena. A further honour came when they were invited to repeat their drive at the RDA's Silver Jubilee Jamboree at Smiths Lawn Windsor in July.

OFFICIALS OF THE HORSLEY GROUPS

Chairmen

Ron Hancock	1969–1975	John Vandeleur-Boorer	1990–1994
Ted Leahey	1975–1979	Colin Wenborn	1994–
Jill Berliand	1979–1986		
Patsie Waugh	1986–1990		

Treasurers

Barron Holroyd	1969–1990	Colin Wenborn	1990–

Secretaries

Gillian Drew	1969–1973	Mary Frise	1989–1991
Stella Hancock	1973–1982	Jane Sugden	1992–1994
Jan Farrant	1982–1987	Philippa Gibson	1994–
Ann Chamberlain	1987–1989		

Physiotherapists
Carolyn Edwards Jones
Patricia Rutter
Elizabeth Homes
Margo Abrahams
Jean Renwick

Horsley Group Main Committee Members

Gilly Blake	1969–1979	Prue Goodchild	1972–1992
Betty Crutchley	1969–1973	Jean Bishop	1973–1976
Anne Creswell	1969–1979	Leslie Smith	1974–1983
Gillian Drew	1969–1974	Jean Pain	1974–1975
Barron Holroyd	1969–1990	Felicity Andrews	1975–1987
Betty Holroyd	1971–1991	Helen Turk	1975–1992
Sue Parker	1969–1979	Shirley Morris	1975–1978
Carol Riley	1969–1978	Sarah Garnett	1976–1980
Rachel Wilson	1969–1970	Sybil Atherton	1976–1991
Terry Thompson	1969–1971	Pam Phillips	1977–1980
Ron Hancock	1969–1984	Kath Stevens	1978–1983
Stella Hancock	1969–1984	Jill Berliand	1978–1983
Christine Isaac	1969–1978	Jan Richards	1979–1988
Ted Leahey	1969–1979	Bridget Harris	1980–1983
Miss M. Price	1969–1970	Helen Croysdill	1980–1984
Paula Stebbing	1970–1991	Mary Crittall	1980–1984
Elizabeth Homes	1971–1973	Valentine Cadell	1981–1985
Margaret Renaud	1971–1974	Jennifer Smith	1981–
June Childs	1973–1975	Frances Johns	1982–1983

Jan Farrant	1982–1989	Janet Sandford	1990–
Diana Cheveley	1983–	Jeremy Ward	1990–1992
Patricia Waugh	1985–1991	Colin Wenborn	1990–
Sonia Windsor	1989–	Philip Royal	1992–
Rosemary Gibb	1989–	Jane Sugden	1992–
Ann Chamberlain	1986–1989	Carry Kurk	1992–
Pippa Jefferey	1987–1989	Colin Gibb	1993–
Vicki Ward	1988–1989	Pauline Brown	1993–
Mary Frise	1989–1992	Carol Redfern	1993–
Jane Lazenby	1990–	Patricia Parker	1993–
John Vandeleur-Boorer	1990–1994	Philippa Gibson	1994–

Driving Group Committee

1977 The inaugural meeting of the Driving Group operating under the Main Committee.
1980 Operating as Group D under the Main Committee.
1983 The Driving Group takes charge of its own finances.
1987 The Driving Group becomes an independent group under its own committee.
1988 The name was changed to The Stella Hancock Driving Group.

Driving Committee Members

Felicity Andrews	1977–1989	Avril Lewis	1985–1994
(Chairman and Organiser)		Pam Le Mottee	1986–1988
Sarah Garnett	1977–1984	(Treasurer 1987 and 1988)	
Stella Hancock	1977–1987	Leslie Ansell	1986–1987
(Secretary and Treasurer)		Brenda May	1987–
Mary Crittall	1977–1987	(Secretary and Organiser)	
Eileen Westerway	1977–1985	Elizabeth Tyas	1989–
Christine Isaac	1977–1978	Helen Pritchard	1989–1994
Madeleine de Garis	1977–1990	Paul Tyas	1990–
Audrey Williams	1978–1987	(Treasurer since 1989)	
Jack Burrill	1978–1986	Ron Fox	1990–1994
Valentine Cadell	1981–1985	(Chairman)	
Sybella McCann	1983–	Beverley Mellstrom	1992–
Milly Millington	1983–1993	Christine David	1993–
Neil Portsmouth	1983–	Judi Ralls	1993–
(Chairman since 1994)			

THE HORSLEY GROUP (FORMERLY WEST HORSLEY)

Group Organisers
Sue Parker, Stella Hancock, Sybil Atherton, Patricia Waugh, Helen Turk, Carol Riley, Jan Richards, Gilly Blake, Paula Stebbing, Prue Goodchild, Jean Bishop, Felicity Andrews, Sonia Windsor, Bridget Harris, Yvonne Fisk, June Hares, Elspeth Watts, Brenda May, Diana Cheveley, Christine Matthews, Garry Kurk.

Group Instructors (Riding and Driving)
Rachel Wilson, Paula Stebbing, Keuke Kilmurry, Barbara Wilson, Gilly Blake, Jean Bishop, Prue Goodchild, June Childs, Patricia Waugh, Sarah Garnett, Jennifer Smith, Diana Cheveley, Helen Croysdill, Leslie Campbell, Joyce Hampton, Helen Turk, Leslie Smith, Felicity Andrews, Jill Robinson, Beverley Mellstrom, Pat Wren, Beverley Mitchell, Audrey Butcher, Avril Lewis, Vicki Ward, Joan Gellatly, Sally Ranger, Anne Parker, Denise Branch, Wendy Westerhoff, Rebecca Gibbon, Barbara Forrest.

The Helpers
Every disabled riding and driving group requires a large number of dedicated people who give their time so willingly to bring happiness and hope to others, many of whom lead very restricted lives.

Here are the names of some who have done so at Horsley during the past 25 years. Mentioning everyone has proved impossible and there are no doubt some whose names have unintentionally been omitted. This does not in any way detract from the contribution they made to the success of the various groups and grateful thanks are also due to them for their dedication and the valuable help they gave.

Sybil Atherton, Sue Allan, Margo Abrahams, Felicity Andrews, Leslie Ansell, Kristine Arena, Claire Axten, Avril Ashworth, Shirley Addison.

Ann Bailey, Sally Bartelf, Amanda Beeham, Georgina Barker, Valerie Belam, Jean Bishop, Lynda Bowsher, Jill Berliand, Sue Baldock, Pauline Brown, Ros Bovill, Sally Broadman, Ann Bates, Pam Begg, Pat Beagley, Gwen Booth, Hilary Bradley, Gilly Blake, Audrey Butcher, Denise Branch, Jack Burrill, Helen Burrill, Jane Bubb, Elizabeth Burke, Janet Bodenham, Katie Breed, members of Bookham Rotaract.

Enid Corbett, Anne Creswell, Ann Chamberlain, Colin Crouch, Deborah Condliffe, Joan Crampton, Dorothy Camm, Diana Cheveley, Sheila Crust, Helen Croysdill, Valantine Cadell, Christine Cook, Mary Crittall, Patricia Coleman, Valerie Cornwall, Gig Cunningham, Catriona Cleary,

June Childs, Leslie Campbell, Betty Crutchley, Claire Cox, Cherry Chidwick, Annette Covey, Roz Clifford.

Pat Dornithorne, Roz Doherty, Mrs M. Deane, Lorna Doaks, Marilyn Derry, Angela Duffin, Dee Derrington, Gillian Drew, Pauline Dilly, Gail Diprose, Christina Elliott, Valerie Ellis, Carolyn Edwards-Jones, Peggy Evans, Janet Ellery.

Elspeth Fletcher, Yvonne Fisk, Norah Felton, Kim Ferrens, Pauline Farino, Gillie Fitzpatrick, Jan Farrant, Mary Frise, Barbara Forrest, Ron Fox, Gillian French.

Mrs J. Gale, Mrs M. Greenside, Rosemary Gibb, Colin Gibb, Tony Gillet, Philippa Gibson, Sue Grobell, Sarah Garnett, Rebecca Gibbon, Madeleine de Garis, Joan Gellatly, Pam Giles, Prue Goodchild, Linda Green.

Betty Holroyd, Jenny Hastead, Helen Harris, Joyce Hampton, June Hares, Jenny Hastend, Jill Herriott, Sarah Hasloch, Brenda Harris, Karleen Hubley, Stella Hancock, Bridget Harris, Elizabeth Homes, Sue Henderson, Sue Holdsworth, Sarah Howison, Valarie Hickmott, Barry Hickmott, Lisa Hickmott.

Julie Jarman, Fiona John, Pippa Jefferey, Frances Johns, Christine Isaac, Marion Jongelie, Gail Jones, Julia Illman, Fleur Johnson, Sue Jones, Helen Inkson, Dorothy Kern, Peter Kern, Mary King, Sue Keville, Magge Kirkham, Keuke Kilmurry, Carry Kurk, Theresa Kelly, Liz Kiddel.

Mrs C. Lemashere, Mrs Lawsen, Carol Londal, Pam Le Mottee, Avril Lewis, Jane Lazenby, Felicity Ledger, Tessa Lee, Angela Lightberry, Jane Lazenby.

Christine Matthews, Anna McNeil, Sybella McCann, Judith Meredith, Juliet Marsh, Beverley Mellstrom, Shirley Morris, Sally MacDougall, Beverley Mitchell, Brenda May, Milly Millington, Carole Manning, Tessa Mann, Gill Miller, Jill Mooratoff, Barbara McGrath.

Anne Noakes, Clare Nealor, Leslie Nightingale, Gill Nesbitt, Mrs R. Nash, Jenny Normald, Shirley Norman, Pam Nellist, Dave Norman, Wendy Olliver, Alec O'Connor, Jean Pain, Pam Phillips, Anne Parker, Pauline Plyford, Joe Pegg, Tessa Pascoe, Linda Page, Sue Parker, Patricia Parker, Helen Pritchard, Maisie Portlock, Chris Peacock.

Joan Renwick, Margaret Renaud, Shirley Radford, Sally Ranger, Mrs Roddam, Mrs Y. Rommer, Janet Rowe, Carol Redfern, Pam Rash,

Maureen Riley, Carol Riley, Jill Robinson, Jan Richards, Jean Renwick, Patricia Rutter, Carole Robinson, Graham Robinson, Judy Raynor, Cathy Renfrey, Philip Royal.

Maureen Sargeant, Barbara Samson, Mrs Shaw, Colin Sandford, Janet Sandford, Jennifer Smith, Julie Snow, Kath Stevens, Frances Spicer, Paula Stebbing, Leslie Smith, Nina Sherry, Anita Smith, Sue Simpson, Jenny Stevenson, Jane Sugden, Hilary Sandon, Elaine Scott, Dorothy Samuels, Carol Snowdon, Jo Sear, Georgina Spencer, Sarah Thomas, Rud Taylor, Helen Turk, Elizabeth Tyas, Paul Tyas, Norman Thomas, Mel Thomas.

Gina Wild, Vicki Ward, Christine Wheatland, Wendy Westerhoff, Mimi Widney, Norah Walker, Terry Wells, Eileen Westerway, Elspeth Watts, Iva de Wilton, Audrey Williams, Rachel Wilson, Patsy Waugh, Sonia Windsor, Vivian Wildman, Muriel Whittock, Barbara Wilson, Pat Wren, Eileen Westerway, David Washbourne, Pattie Williamson, Jennifer Williames, Elizabeth Vandeleur-Boorer.

The Horses and Ponies
The patience and willingness shown by the horses and ponies being ridden and driven at Horsley, by disabled people of all ages, has at times been quite remarkable. Here are the names of some who have done such valient service to the various groups over the years.

Beech Nut, Mousie, Dimple, Conker, Sainsbury's Prince, Twanger, Zephair, Golden Oriel, Blackie, Pepper, Jason, Ben, Coleen, Merrylegs, Miner, Nutkin, Cobweb, Riley, Rotary Albert, Dumpling, Burgundy, Sunshine, Justin, Little John, Taffy, Christopher Robin, Star, Miss Muffett, Mork, Dinky, Red Rascal, Shandy, Tittlemouse, Bubbly, Harry, Flash, Pebbles, Sinbad, Sonny, Gypsey, Punch, Amber, Napoleon, Sabastian, Gilbert, Bertz, Magic, Marmeduke, Aaron, Rosie, William, Spud, Maxie, Harley, Toppa, Soloway, Candy, Pudding, Rocky, Sandy Robin, Dewi, Shadow.

They have been the real stars at Horsley.